"'The Spirit clearly says that in later times some will abandon the faith and follow deceiving spirits and things taught by demons' (1 Tim. 4:1 NIV). That is presently happening all over the world, and pastors, disciplers, and counselors are waking up to that reality and learning how to set captives free. Steve Dabbs discovered this when he was a chaplain in the military and shares his learning and experiences in this helpful book that you should read and add to your library."

Dr. Neil T. Anderson, founder and president emeritus of Freedom in Christ Ministries

"Steve Dabbs's new book, When Demons Surface, is a very readable introduction to the topic of spiritual warfare. He gives abundant evidence of what the Bible says about Satan and demons and also draws copiously on extrabiblical sources from the ancient world on the subject. Along the way, he shares many encounters with demons from his work in ministry. This book is a worthy contribution to the literature on a biblical calling that the church needs to understand and, when appropriate, engage in."

Jeffrey J. Niehaus, PhD, senior professor of Old Testament, Gordon-Conwell Theological Seminary; author of numerous books and articles on biblical theology; and contributor to The Kingdom and the Power

"Steve wrote a much-needed book sharing his incredible experience based on a careful understanding of the biblical reality and danger of demonic forces. His expert analysis of the biblical languages coupled with historical context will challenge and inform modern ideas on the subject as well as open eyes and hearts to the spiritual battle raging in our world today."

Hobert K. Farrell, PhD, professor emeritus of biblical studies, LeTourneau University

"This book is a valuable resource and road map on the quest for finding freedom in Christ. The reader will explore gripping stories about demons and delve into meticulous research as Chaplain Dabbs fearlessly exposes the cunning tactics of sinister forces at play. The Christian, clergy, and counselor alike will gain valuable insights into the ancient biblical art of confronting evil spirits in the mighty Name of Jesus."

Dr. Anthony L. Wiggins, chaplain, Lieutenant Colonel, US Air Force

TRUE STORIES OF SPIRITUAL WARFARE

WHEN

AND WHAT THE BIBLE SAYS

DEMONS

ABOUT CONFRONTING THE DARKNESS

SURFACE

STEVE DABBS

BakerBooks

a division of Baker Publishing Group
Grand Rapids, Michigan

Published by Baker Books
a division of Baker Publishing Group
Grand Rapids, Michigan
BakerBooks.com

Printed in the United States of America

Library of Congress Cataloging-in-Publication Data
Names: Dabbs, Steve, author.
Title: When demons surface : true stories of spiritual warfare and what the Bible says about confronting the darkness / Steve Dabbs.
Description: Grand Rapids, Michigan : Baker Books, a division of Baker Publishing Group, [2024] | Includes bibliographical references.
Identifiers: LCCN 2024005418 | ISBN 9781540904119 (paper) | ISBN 9781540904171 (casebound) | ISBN 9781493445738 (ebook)
Subjects: LCSH: Spiritual warfare. | Spiritual warfare—Biblical teaching.
Classification: LCC BV4509.5 .D195 2024 | DDC 235/.4—dc23/eng/20240226
LC record available at https://lccn.loc.gov/2024005418

24 25 26 27 28 29 30   7 6 5 4 3 2 1

Dedicated to
PASTOR BILLY MACK HILL SR.
(November 8, 1956–December 18, 2023)
You gave me my first instruction
on spiritual warfare.

CONTENTS

PART 1

PERSONAL ENCOUNTERS

13 TRUE STORIES

1

THE REALM OF DARKNESS DISPELLED BY THE LIGHT

The first humans experienced spiritual warfare from the very first book of the Bible, shortly after the start of their very existence (Gen. 3:1). From the Creation to the Judgment, Satan actively wages war against us (Rev. 20:1–10). Christ sanctioned the ministry of confronting demons to establish His kingdom and to provide relief to those suffering in spiritual battle (Luke 10:1–18; 11:20).

In this book, I share over 50 true stories, including instances of demonization and paranormal activities. They also involve cases of physical and mental health issues that shockingly proved to have an evil spirit as their source. I divide the book into three parts:

1. Personal Encounters
2. Biblical Insights
3. Pastoral Experiences

With Scripture as our authority, I ultimately rely on the biblical languages of Hebrew and Greek for an accurate handling of the truth. As the renowned scholar Dr. Gordon D. Fee taught, "The very nature of Scripture demands that the [researcher] have some skills in investigating the historical-cultural background of the [Bible]."[1] Thus, I include ancient Jewish and early church writings originating during or close to the biblical times. In doing so, *I uncover what is old and teach nothing new*.

The Bible warns that the modern age will bring an *increase* in demonic activity as people "abandon the faith and follow deceiving spirits and things taught by demons" (1 Tim. 4:1 NIV). Therefore, my intent is to expose ways demons strive to infiltrate our lives and to equip believers to successfully combat them.

THE INITIAL ENCOUNTER THAT PROMPTED THIS

It took 10 years before I initially shared this story. I grew up in a Christian home, and I was baptized at the age of eight. As a junior in high school, I was no longer attending church. I bused tables at a restaurant on the weekends.

My best friend, Allen Gill, had an annoying habit of asking me on Saturday nights if I would attend church with him on Sunday. I couldn't avoid him because he was my ride home from work. I turned him down every week—until he told me, "Man, my church is where many of the high school girls go."

I replied, "Why didn't you tell me that earlier? Pick me up in the morning!"

1. Gordon D. Fee, *New Testament Exegesis*, rev. ed. (Louisville: Westminster John Knox, 1993), 114. The words in brackets are to clarify "researcher" instead of "exegete" and "Bible" instead of "NT text." The same rules of hermeneutics apply to the Old Testament.

After several weeks of attending church, God started softly tugging at my heart. I knew God loved me, but I had no holy fear of Him—respect, yes, but fear, no. The conviction to rededicate my life to Christ became a nuisance. Instead of wooing me, God angered me.

MY HELLFIRE EXPERIENCE

One Saturday afternoon before heading to work, I decided it was high time to call a meeting with God. I walked swiftly into my bedroom, shut the door, pointed my hand in a commanding way toward heaven, and told God, "Here's the deal!" And I went on to tell Him that if He wanted my soul, I was willing to give up particular sins of no interest to me, but "I reserve the right to 'chase girls.'" Then I rushed out of the room, slammed the door behind me, and left God in my room to think about it.

I came home from work around 11 p.m., took a shower, arranged my clothes for church, then climbed into bed. Around 3 a.m. that Sunday, God answered me in a supernatural vision. In the vision, I was having sex with a beautiful girl. Then all of a sudden, the girl disappeared, the bed disappeared, the entire floor opened up like a trapdoor, and I fell into a lake of fire. I was awakened by my tormented screams.

God's reply was dramatic and clear—"No deal!"

The next morning, Allen came to pick me up for church. When he walked into my bedroom, he was speechless as he watched me shoving pornographic magazines along with numerous letters and pictures from high school girls into a huge black trash bag. He reached for one of the magazines, and I slapped his hand, snatched it from him, and shoved it

13

back into the trash bag. As we walked to his car, I dropped the double-tied trash bag at the curb for Monday's garbage pickup, and we were silent the whole drive to church. I didn't dare tell Allen about the vision, but he knew something had happened to me.

HOW FEAR AND LOVE ARE RELATED

King Solomon instructs, "The fear of the LORD is the beginning of knowledge" (Prov. 1:7). Jesus teaches, "Love the Lord your God with all your heart and with all your soul and with all your mind" (Matt. 22:37 NIV).[2] The Apostle Paul commands believers to "continue to work out your salvation with fear and trembling" (Phil. 2:12 NIV). The Apostle John teaches, "There is no fear in love; but perfect love casts out fear" (1 John 4:18a NASB). So which one is it, love or fear? It's both. The Bible declares, "Notice how God is both kind and severe. He is severe toward those who disobeyed, but kind to you if you continue to trust in his kindness. But if you stop trusting, you also will be cut off" (Rom. 11:22 NLT).

Regarding 1 John 4:18a, the Apostle John is discussing Christian assurance. He finishes the verse with "fear involves punishment, and the one who fears is not perfected in love" (4:18b NASB). For clarity, he states earlier in the same book, "Whoever keeps [God's] word, in him the love of God has truly been perfected"[3] (1 John 2:5 NASB). Jesus Himself con-

2. Jesus also taught, "And do not fear those who kill the body but cannot kill the soul. But rather fear Him who is able to destroy both soul and body in hell" (Matt. 10:28 NKJV).

3. Greek: τέλειος (teleios), "mature, complete, fulfilled, or perfect," per Walter Bauer, A Greek-English Lexicon of the New Testament and Other Early Christian

firms this when He insists, "If you love Me, keep My commandments" (John 14:15 NKJV). In other words, the Apostle John assures believers that if they have perfected their love for God by living an obedient life, then they have no need to fear being punished by Him.[4] Putting it all together, the fear of being punished by God should lead the disobedient to repent and the obedient to *remain* repentant.[5]

As for me, I experienced that fearful vision because I was on the wrong side of God. Yet He loved me enough to give me a wake-up call. Again, I always knew God loved me, but I did not reciprocate that love until I comprehended the Gospel—that God the Father hates sin so much He sent His Son to die in the place of sinners to satisfy His own wrath, and it was His love for humanity that motivated Him to do so (Rom. 5:6–11).

NOT ALL SINS ARE THE SAME

I didn't realize I was doing anything really wrong compared to everyone else. Well, I knew premarital sex was a sin, but aren't all sins the same? After that terrifying vision, I started reading my Bible for the first time. It all made sense when I came across these three Scriptures:

Literature, ed. Frederick W. Danker, 3rd ed. (Chicago: University of Chicago Press, 2000), entry 6336; hereafter DANK.

4. Additionally, this view is confirmed by the Apostle John stating earlier that obedience is evidence of "how we know we are [abiding] in him" (1 John 2:5 NIV), combined with the emphasis in 1 John 4:17 on abiding in God as evidence of "how love is made complete [perfect] among us so that we will have confidence on the day of judgment" (NIV).

5. Greek: μετανοέω (*metanoeō*), "have a serious change of mind and heart about a previous point of view or course of behavior" (DANK, 4210). It's a compound verb from *meta* (change) and *noeō* (thinking).

1. "Do not be deceived! Neither sexually immoral people, nor idolaters, nor adulterers, nor passive homosexual partners,[6] nor dominant homosexual partners,[7] nor thieves, nor greedy persons, not drunkards, not [verbally] abusive persons,[8] not swindlers will inherit the kingdom of God" (1 Cor. 6:9–10 LEB).

2. "The acts of the flesh are obvious: sexual immorality, impurity and debauchery; idolatry and witchcraft; hatred, discord, jealousy, fits of rage, selfish ambition, dissensions, factions and envy; drunkenness, orgies, and the like. I warn you, as I did before, that those who live like this will not inherit the kingdom of God" (Gal. 5:19–21 NIV).

3. "But the cowardly, the unbelieving, the vile, the murderers, the sexually immoral, those who practice magic arts, the idolaters and all liars—they will be consigned to the fiery lake of burning sulfur. This is the second death" (Rev. 21:8 NIV).

Why does the Bible warn us, "Do not be deceived" (1 Cor. 6:9)? It's because many people are deceived into thinking they can make a lifestyle of these sins and still go to heaven. Galatians 5:21 even adds the phrase "and the like" (NIV) to cover other behaviors from which people must repent.

---

6. Greek: μαλακός (*malakos*), the effeminate participant in same-sex intercourse (DANK, 4071).

7. Greek: ἀρσενοκοίτης (*arsenokoitēs*), the dominant participant in same-sex intercourse (DANK, 931).

8. Greek: λοίδορος (*loidoros*), "one who abuses another with speech," per Timothy Friberg, Barbara Friberg, and Neva F. Miller, *Analytical Lexicon to the Greek New Testament* (Grand Rapids: Baker Books, 2000), entry 17453; hereafter Friberg.

The forbidden behaviors in the scriptural lists above are known as "Second Death Sins."[9] This category is derived by combining the Apostle John's teachings where he refers to:

1. Sins leading to death versus sins not leading to death (1 John 5:16–17); and
2. Sins leading to the "second death" (Rev. 21:8).

Also, Jesus declared that Judas was "guilty of a greater sin" (John 19:11 NIV), further validating there are lesser sins too.

Now take another glance at the New Testament lists of Second Death Sins. Notice that idolatry and sexual immorality are the only two sins repeated. This is because they're inextricably linked throughout the Bible. The Old Testament records them as two major sins that pollute the land (Lev. 18:24–27; Jer. 3:1–2, 9).[10] Many practices of idolatry included ritual sex (1 Kings 14:24; 2 Kings 23:7; Hosea 4:14). Additionally, the Greek construction of Colossians 3:5 defines all sexual sins—including acts of defilement, lust, evil desire, and

---

9. Some Christian traditions use the term *mortal sins*, meaning "deadly sins."

10. Dr. Jeffrey J. Niehaus notes the Old Testament teaches that the land is polluted by three main sins—idolatry, sexual immorality, and murder. (See his *Biblical Theology*, vol. 1 [Bellingham, WA: Lexham Press, 2014], 213–14.) Regarding murder, Moses teaches, "Bloodshed pollutes the land" (Num. 35:33 NIV). Likewise, when Cain killed Abel, his younger brother, God declared, "The voice of your brother's blood is crying to me from the ground" (Gen. 4:10).

Although two of the New Testament lists on Second Death Sins written by the Apostle Paul do not include "murder" (1 Cor. 6:9–10; Gal. 5:19–21), that sin can be implied by (1) his phrase "and the like" (Gal. 5:21 NIV); and (2) the New Testament's allusions to these Old Testament prohibitions.

Moreover, Dr. Niehaus adds, "If we consider that the three major categories of sin connected with pollution of the land/world are sexual sins, idolatry, and murder, we see that the eschatological indictment that 'the earth lies polluted under its inhabitants' is foreshadowed and has indeed been earned by every society that has ever existed after the Fall" (214).

insatiability—as idolatry. Moreover, Romans 1:18–32 traces how a society devolves from idol worship to full-blown sexual deviancy.

As an additional insight, God consistently refers to believers as His bride.[11] This is why He metaphorically equates idolatry to adultery.[12] Building on that fact, 1 John 5:18–20 uses specific Greek verbs to describe unbelievers "reclining with"[13] and being "touched by"[14] the evil one, painting a disturbing picture of their "sexual" relationship.[15] Coincidentally, verse 21 abruptly ends the letter commanding believers to "keep yourselves from idols."

May God forbid that anyone be confused about sexual sins—like I was—because our eternity is at stake. For our well-being, the New Testament provides once-and-for-all clarity on the subject of sexuality. Remember, Jesus entrusted the Apostles with the writing of the New Testament.[16] So the Apostles are the ones who safeguarded the Gospel (Gal.

---

11. Isa. 54:5–6; Hosea 2:16–20; Eph. 5:25–27; Rev. 19:7–8.

12. Ps. 106:37–39; Isa. 57:7–9; Jer. 3:9; Ezek. 23:37.

13. Greek: κεῖμαι (keimai), to lie down or be in a set or relaxed position (DANK, 3632).

14. Greek: ἅπτω (haptō), to touch or to have sexual relations (1 Cor. 7:1) (DANK, 861).

15. See my expanded analysis in chap. 6, "15 Points of Clarity about Expelling Demons," point 15. Also, notice how the Bible applies the imagery of forbidden human sexuality to believers (God's bride) worshiping idols:

    a. "Why . . . fondle the breasts of a promiscuous woman?" (Prov. 5:20 NLT).

    b. "[Samaria and Jerusalem] became prostitutes in Egypt. Even as young girls, they allowed men to fondle their breasts. . . . I married them, and they bore me sons and daughters. Then [Samaria] lusted after other lovers instead of me . . . so she prostituted herself with the most desirable men of Assyria, worshiping their idols and defiling herself. . . . Yet even though [Jerusalem] saw what had happened to [Samaria], her sister, she followed right in her footsteps . . . defiling herself just like her older sister" (Ezek. 23:3–5, 7, 11, 13 NLT).

16. Matt. 28:19–20; John 21:24–25; 2 Pet. 3:15–16.

1:8–9), established the church (Eph. 2:19–20), and developed the rules for Christian living (Acts 2:42). In Acts 15, all the Apostles meet in Jerusalem to hold a council to determine which Old Testament commandments are still required for New Covenant believers. They unanimously agree:

> The Holy Spirit has led us to the decision that no burden [besides the teachings of Christ] should be placed on you other than these essentials: refuse food offered to idols, [forbidden matters related to] blood, the meat from strangled animals, and *sexual immorality*. You will do well to *avoid such things*. (Acts 15:28–29 CEB, brackets added for full clarity)

This means Christians must obey all Old Testament commandments related to sexuality, which include avoiding adultery, homosexuality, bestiality, and incest (Lev. 18:1–30; 20:10–23). In short, no one is allowed to have sex except for a married, monogamous, heterosexual couple (Gen. 2:21–24; Matt. 19:3–6; 1 Cor. 7:2).

THE DARKNESS SURFACED AFTER I SAW THE LIGHT

At first I didn't know I was in spiritual darkness—until I had a terrifying vision that led me to submit to the Lordship of Jesus Christ. After that, a dark presence started visiting my bedroom in the middle of the night. I also started experiencing sleep paralysis and being startled out of my sleep by an invisible hand around my throat.

However, who could I tell? My church never taught about these issues. Others led me to believe evil spirits can't bother a Christian in these ways.

When I later entered full-time ministry as a military chaplain, people from every background and walk of life came to me for pastoral care. Periodically, while in the privacy of a counseling session as I was aiding a person through an unresolved issue, a demonic personality would shockingly surface in them. Eventually, I shook off my uncomfortableness with the subject of spiritual warfare and started teaching on it. To my surprise, I met people from teenagers to senior citizens and from junior employees to senior leaders who had similar encounters with demons. This less-spoken-of reality prompted me to write about it.

WHY WE SHOULD BE CONCERNED ABOUT SPIRITUAL WARFARE

If Christians are exempt from Satan's attacks, why does the Apostle Paul warn us on three separate occasions to put on the full armor of God (Rom. 13:12; Eph. 6:11, 13; 1 Thess. 5:8)? Also, if Jesus has all power, why should we be concerned about spiritual warfare? Here are five more reasons we must prepare to engage in spiritual battles:

1. Satan is defeated but not yet destroyed (Rev. 20:10).
2. Satan and his demons wage war against us (Eph. 6:12).
3. Jesus commands us to pray daily for protection from the evil one (Matt. 6:13).
4. God directs us to know Satan's tactics to avoid being exploited by him (2 Cor. 2:11).
5. God orders us to remain alert against demonic attacks (1 Pet. 5:8).

Regarding the spiritual armor, there are six components (Eph. 6:14–17). Two enable preparation (*belt* of truth and *footwear* of peace), and three offer protection (*breastplate* of righteousness, *shield* of faith, *helmet* of salvation). However, only one is a weapon (the *sword* of God's Word). This sword is *not* the long one you typically see warriors dueling with in historical movies. The Greek identifies it as a dagger used in hand-to-hand combat.[17]

The dagger metaphor introduces some fascinating theology. We are reminded our battle with the evil one will be up close and personal. It also implies that even a "little" knowledge of the Bible is an effective weapon against the enemy. For example, Jesus replied to Satan's three temptations with a stab each time using short quotes of Scripture (Matt. 4:1–11).

SATAN INTRODUCED THE DARKNESS

How did humanity fall into the predicament of spiritual darkness? The book of Genesis tells us Adam and Eve were clueless about evil before they disobeyed God. When the devil tempted them, Adam and Eve ate from the "Tree of the Knowledge of Good and Evil." Immediately after they ate that forbidden fruit, the whole world became shrouded in spiritual darkness.

God's kind footsteps were replaced with thunderclaps and His peaceful presence with a foreboding storm.[18] *The*

17. Greek: μάχαιρα (*machaira*), a small sword or dagger; a weapon for close combat; also a large knife for killing and cutting up an animal (Friberg, 17892).
18. Jeffrey J. Niehaus, "In the Wind of the Storm: Another Look at Genesis III 8," *Vetus Testamentum* 44, no. 2 (1994): 263–67. The traditional and incorrect translation has they "heard the sound of the LORD walking in the cool of the day."

Dictionary of Classical Hebrew accepts the correct translation of Genesis 3:8 as "[Adam and Eve] heard the thunder of Yahweh God as he was going back and forth in the garden in the wind of the storm."[19] The theological picture is that God took an adversarial stance against Adam and Eve after they disobeyed Him.

We are spiritual beings who live in a physical body. God is the source of spiritual life. Separation from God causes spiritual death. Thus, when Adam and Eve disobeyed God, He separated them from His presence, resulting in an instant spiritual death and a countdown to physical death. Since then, all humans are born genetically predisposed to disobey God. We stumble around in spiritual darkness, unsure of where we're going, hurting ourselves and others along the way, and many times walking past those in pain all around us.[20]

JESUS DISPELLED THE DARKNESS

Before God banished Adam and Eve from the garden of Eden, He promised to send His Son, Jesus, to crush the head of the devil by atoning for the sins of the world.[21]

Until the promised arrival of Jesus, God chose to selectively reveal Himself. He enacted a plan to redeem the world by creating the nation of Israel from the lineage of Abraham.[22] He freed them from Egyptian slavery, brought them to Mount Sinai, and gave them a new set of commandments. Yet He hid His presence in a thunderstorm, as with Adam

19. David J. A. Clines, ed., *The Dictionary of Classical Hebrew*, vol. 4 (Sheffield: Sheffield Academic Press, 1998), 185.

20. Eccles. 7:29; 12:13; Mic. 6:8; Rom. 3:23; 5:12; 6:23.

21. Gen. 3:15; Rom. 5:8; 10:9; 16:20; Col. 2:15.

22. Gen. 17:5; Exod. 32:13; Rom. 4:13.

and Eve.[23] Those who obeyed God were called "the children of light" and assigned to be a ray of hope to the rest of the nations walking in darkness.[24]

Although God chose to dwell among the nation of Israel, He still restricted His presence to a 15-by-15-foot section of a tent—the tabernacle. When they eventually moved worship into the temple, the size of the section doubled to 30 by 30 feet.[25] This small room was the only flicker of true light in a vast world shrouded in spiritual darkness. Moreover, this most holy space could be entered only once a year by one person—the high priest (Heb. 9:6–7).

Centuries later, Jesus, the Light of the World (John 8:12; 9:5; Rev. 22:5), came to dispel the darkness. The moment He atoned for our sins by His death on the cross, history records that the curtain in the temple restricting access to the most holy place was torn in two from top to bottom (Matt. 27:51). Now all who submit to His Lordship can go right into the presence of God.[26]

THE CHURCH CONFRONTS THE DARKNESS

Jesus successfully contended with the army of darkness. "He disarmed the spiritual rulers and authorities. He shamed them publicly by his victory over them on the cross" (Col. 2:15 NLT). Afterward, He ascended back to heaven and will return on the last day.[27] In the meantime, He empowers the

23. Exod. 12:51; 19:17–19; 20:18.
24. See Isa. 49:6 and Qumran Scrolls sections I and III, from Millar Burrows, *The Dead Sea Scrolls* (New York: Viking Press, 1956), 390–92.
25. Exod. 26:16; 40:34–38; 2 Chron. 3:8.
26. Rom. 5:12–21; 10:9–10; Heb. 2:14; 10:22.
27. Acts 1:9–11; 1 Thess. 4:15–17; Heb. 4:14; Rev. 19:11–21; 20:7–15.

"children of light"[28] to advance His kingdom by sharing the Gospel of truth (Eph. 1:13) and freeing all others trapped in the realm of darkness.[29]

Satan still blinds the eyes of those in desperate need of the light of the Gospel (2 Cor. 4:4).[30] As we strive to reach them, the Apostle Paul warns that we'll inevitably engage in spiritual battle—subtly or overtly:

> We use God's mighty weapons, not worldly weapons, to knock down the strongholds of human reasoning and to destroy false arguments. We destroy every proud obstacle that keeps people from knowing God. We capture their rebellious thoughts and teach them to obey Christ. (2 Cor. 10:4–5 NLT)

We're reminded that the battlefield is the mind. Deception remains Satan's number one tactic, since he's the "father of lies" (John 8:44). Therefore, most of our spiritual battles will be truth encounters. Here's one:

- LIE: "They sold their souls to the devil."
- TRUTH: God claims, "All souls are mine" (Ezek. 18:4)—even Satan's soul (Rev. 20:10).

True freedom can be obtained only by submitting to the Lordship of Jesus Christ. This is why He Himself declares,

---

28. Eph. 5:8; 1 Thess. 5:5. See other references to "light" (Matt. 5:14; Col. 1:12; 1 Pet. 2:9). See also Acts 11:26 for the first time Jesus's followers are called "Christians."

29. Matt. 28:18–20; Col. 1:13.

30. Ezek. 18:32; Acts 17:26–28; Rom. 10:14–17; Eph. 2:2; 2 Pet. 3:9. Also, *Gospel* means "good news," consisting of Jesus dying for our sins (Good Friday) and rising from the dead three days later (Easter Sunday) (see 1 Cor. 15:3–4).

"the truth will set you free" and "I am . . . the truth" (John 8:32; 14:6).

In conclusion, as the title *When Demons Surface* implies, occasions will arise requiring us to exercise our authority in Christ by confronting evil spirits. But do not fear, because Jesus promises, "I have given you authority to trample on snakes and scorpions and to overcome all the power of the enemy; nothing will harm you" (Luke 10:19 NIV). So, with confidence, let us dispel the darkness with the light of Christ![31]

31. 2 Cor. 4:4–6; 2 Tim. 1:10.

2

CONFRONTING THE SHADOW CREATURE

My wife and I took our teenagers Black Friday shopping every year, so they could maximize their clothing and Christmas allowances. My family knew my participation was an act of great love, because I hate shopping.

After hours of walking around the mall, I rallied the family for a break in the food court. There was a man whose face was hidden behind a newspaper. To give him privacy, I sat at a table a few feet away and had my teenagers sit at another table that was in view of the man and me. Two of my teenagers tried to get my attention by signaling with their mouths and patting their seats. However, I beckoned for them to quiet down so they wouldn't disturb the man.

After we finished our break, I stood up to continue the laborious journey of shopping. When we got about 10 feet away, my children stopped me: "Dad, didn't you realize we were trying to get your attention? The second you sat down, that man lowered his newspaper and began to snarl and growl at you!"

By then I had been in ministry for over 20 years and had grown accustomed to this kind of thing. As a side effect of expelling demons, occasionally people in public give me spontaneous angry looks.

The Bible tells the story of some non-Christians who tried to cast out demons "in the name of Jesus, whom Paul preaches." However, on one occasion "the evil spirit replied, 'I know Jesus, and I know Paul, but who are you?' Then the man with the evil spirit leaped on them, overpowered them, and attacked them with such violence that they fled from the house, naked and battered" (Acts 19:13, 15–16 NLT). The evil spirit knew the Apostle Paul, because he was submitted to the Lordship of Jesus Christ. And that is how evil spirits know me—and even you, if Christ is your Lord.

As another example, early in my ministry, I was counseling a young lady. Shortly into our session, her eyes widened, and she stiffened her back, stood up, and walked backward out of the office. I followed her into the hallway and asked her what happened.

She spoke through her teeth, "The demon told me to leave your office—now!"

I convinced her to come back, but as soon as we resumed, she started smiling—in a weird way. So I asked her, "What's going on?"

She said, "The demon is laughing at you."

Not knowing what to do, I said a quick prayer and ended the session. The demon knew me, because I know Christ. Yet the demon also knew I was truly naive about the power and authority of Christ that resides in me (Luke 9:1). I would soon learn, and the demons would regret it.

FIGHTING A WAR I DID NOT KNOW EXISTED

As I was growing up, I didn't know much about God. So you can understand why I believed, "If you don't bother the devil, he's not going to bother you." For most of my life, it appeared to be true. I was a typical unchurched high school junior. I lived in sin, cussed on occasion, and watched horror movies. However, I never had any demonic encounters—until I gave my life to Christ.

When I had that frightful vision of falling into hell, I woke up that Sunday at 3 a.m., sat up in my bed startled, and in the pitch darkness of my bedroom rededicated my life to Christ. Later that morning, the strangest thing happened at the end of the church service. I recall actually remembering a sermon for the first time. My desires changed—well, I redirected my desires. It wasn't like I didn't want to do those sinful things anymore—I was *afraid* to do them. Though my circle of friends dwindled due to my changed life, I had unexplainable peace and joy like never before.

Then came the visits. One night, I was awakened by a force pressing against my chest. It was uncomfortable, but after a minute or so, it stopped, and I went back to sleep. This happened a couple more nights, and then it escalated. I was startled out of my sleep by a hand around my neck. I reached out but felt no arm.

Eventually, I was able to gasp, "Ga-ga-God, hep-hep-help me!" The pressure on my neck immediately stopped. I instantly knew this was an evil spirit, but who was I going to tell?

FIGHTING IN THE DARK

I had always heard that demons are creatures of the dark and don't like the light, so I went to the store and purchased a night-light. That made it worse. This time when I was attacked in my sleep, I looked up and saw what it was—a fierce shadow creature. I woke up every few minutes throughout the night.

Obviously, the night-light wasn't emitting enough brightness, so I started sleeping with the TV on. By the glow of the TV, I looked up and saw the shadow creature staring down at me. As you can guess, the night visits intensified.

The encounters started happening even in the daytime when I took naps due to the lack of sleep from the night visits. During every encounter, I would pray and the episode would end—until the enemy caught on to this and began to cover my mouth. I truly reached a point of crisis when one evening I felt my mattress shift, and when I opened my eyes, I was levitating about six feet above the floor.

I pretended to remain sleeping, prayed under my breath, and I felt the mattress return to the box spring. I grew up in the inner city, and I know what it's like to be bullied. I was being spiritually bullied, but like with any bully, you have to learn how to righteously fight back.

I mustered up the courage to speak to a trusted pastor and friend (Billy Hill). For fear of being mislabeled, I didn't share everything—especially about the levitation—but I gave him enough examples to assure him I wasn't making this up.

He thought for a moment, then quipped, "Steve, your problem is you don't know who you are. You need to memorize some Scriptures about your identity and authority in Christ so you can end these battles." He jotted down a few Scriptures, handed the list to me, then changed the subject.

I nodded in agreement, but I felt insulted. I was looking for pity, not a pep talk.

Now, after 35 years of military service, I understand this to be warrior talk. As Dr. Neil T. Anderson declares, "Some are pleading, 'O God, please help us! The devil is roaring at us!' And God responds, 'I've done all I'm going to do. I defeated and disarmed Satan at the cross. I conferred all authority on you in Christ. Now open your eyes. Realize who you are and start living accordingly.'"[1]

This is when I started hitting the gym of God's Word, for "physical training is good, but training for godliness is much better, promising benefits in this life and in the life to come" (1 Tim. 4:8 NLT).

PREPARING FOR BATTLE!

The Bible describes spiritual warfare as:

1. Hand-to-hand combat;
2. Against an enemy who is evil, nonhuman, with superior abilities, and not from this world; and
3. A battle in our favor—if we fight back with the dagger of God's Word.

1. Neil T. Anderson, *The Bondage Breaker* (Eugene, OR: Harvest House, 2000), 85.

The dagger is a perfect biblical metaphor for Scripture, for it confirms why Jesus responded with one-sentence scriptural stabs to each of Satan's temptations.

Additionally, I later learned:

1. Jesus defeated Satan and his demons at the cross (Col. 2:14–15);
2. We are spiritually seated with Jesus in heaven when we submit to His Lordship (Eph. 2:6);
3. Jesus grants us authority to expel demons (Luke 10:19);
4. We must rely on the power of God to expel demons (Luke 11:20; John 15:5); and
5. God's power enables us to take our stand and resist the devil (Eph. 6:11; 1 Pet. 5:8–9).

However, let us pick up where we left off when I was a teenaged believer seeking help regarding the shadow creature. I memorized the Scriptures from the list Pastor Billy gave me. I still recall three:

1. I am more than a conqueror through Jesus Christ (Rom. 8:37).
2. No weapon formed against me shall prosper (Isa. 54:17).
3. Greater is He who lives in me than the devil who is in the world (1 John 4:4).

Then I waited.

The first night passed, and nothing happened. The second night went by, but still nothing—then a third, a fourth, and a whole week passed. One night when I least expected it, I felt a presence in the room. I looked up and saw the shadow creature standing in front of the glow of the TV.

He started approaching me. I began to tremble. But I knew "courage isn't the absence of fear but bravery in the midst of it!"[2] So I sat up in my bed, and with tears in my eyes I began to declare, "I am more than a conqueror through Jesus Christ my Lord! Greater is He that is in me than he that's in the world! No weapon formed against me shall prosper!"

Every time I quoted Scripture, the shadow creature winced. Then I pointed my finger and ordered, "In the Name of Jesus, I command you to leave my room!" Immediately, it left! Afterward, I sat in my bed and wept in victory.

WE MUST FIGHT!

As God led the Israelites to the border of the ancient promised land, He assured Joshua, "Every place on which the sole of your foot treads, I have given it to you" (Josh. 1:3 NASB), but they still had to fight (v. 11).

Before Jesus was crucified, He proclaimed to His disciples, "I will build my church, and the gates of hell shall not prevail against it" (Matt. 16:18b), but they were still resisted (Acts 4:18).

After His resurrection, Jesus declared, "All authority in heaven and on earth has been given to me. Therefore go"

2. Similar versions are attributed to President Franklin D. Roosevelt, Nelson Mandela, C. S. Lewis, and others.

(Matt. 28:18–19 NIV), but believers are still persecuted (2 Tim. 3:12).

Although our almighty God secured our victory, He still prepares us to obtain it through battle. I won the battle that night, but the war did not end.

3

ENDING NIGHTMARES AND SLEEP PARALYSIS BY AN ANCIENT PRAYER

In the days after successfully confronting the shadow creature, I was riding high. Shortly afterward, something else took its place. I occasionally awoke from terrible nightmares. To make matters worse, I experienced sleep paralysis several times a week. During the episode, I felt an invisible hand around my neck and a hand cup my mouth to prevent me from praying.

I discovered a biblical answer that helped me finally rid myself of nightmares and sleep paralysis. It has worked for my Christian clients too.

NIGHT DEMONS ATTACKED OLD TESTAMENT BELIEVERS

Bible scholar Dr. Marvin R. Wilson laments, "The Church has neglected its Jewish heritage to its own detriment."[1] Coinci-

---

1. Marvin R. Wilson, *Our Father Abraham: Jewish Roots of the Christian Faith*, 2nd ed. (Grand Rapids: Eerdmans, 2021), 34.

dentally, I found answers to my spiritual battles only when I researched ancient Jewish history. Afterward, I was conflicted. On the one hand, I was relieved—"Thank God it's not just me!" On the other hand, I was disappointed—"How could the church lose this much connection to its historical roots?"

For example, ancient Jews believed "night is the time of demons."[2] Due to their experiences, they had grave concerns about midnight. For them, it is the midpoint of the evening— a two-hour period six hours after sundown.[3] If sundown is 9 p.m., then the midpoint of the night is 3 a.m., known also in our day as the "bewitching hour."[4]

They believed this time period fostered increased danger, mischief, and demonic attacks—including nightmares. In response, they were encouraged to awake during this time to pray and recite scriptural truths so that "demons stay away from" them.[5] Even King David followed this practice: "At midnight I rise to give you thanks for your righteous laws" (Ps. 119:62 NIV).

2. Babylonian Talmud (hereafter BT), Avot 3.4.2. Also, this is validated in:
 a. Archaeology: "Like bandits [demons] raid human habitations, especially during the night; they seize people . . . and spread illness . . . they lie in wait for a passing traveler" (Daniel Schwemer, "Demons, Demonology," in *The Encyclopedia of the Bible and Its Reception*, vol. 6, *Dabbesheth— Dreams and Dream Interpretation* [Berlin: de Gruyter, 2012], 534).
 b. Modern counseling testimonies: "The good news is that most direct attacks occur at night and when you are alone, so verbally resisting Satan won't be a matter of public spectacle" (Anderson, *Bondage Breaker*, 101).

3. Likutei Moharan 149.1.4: "And the main time for Chatzot [midpoint of the night] is always six hours from nightfall, whether in summer or winter. The time of Chatzot begins then, and continues until the end of the second watch—i.e., for two hours."

4. René Ostberg, "Witching Hour," *Britannica*, November 30, 2022, https:// www.britannica.com/topic/witching-hour.

5. BT, Berakhot 5a.5. The specific Scripture is the Shema found in Deut. 6:4–9; 11:13–21; Num. 15:37–41.

It seems strange to us that people actually arose at midnight to pray—until we discover that up to the 1800s, civilizations generally observed two four-hour periods of sleep.[6] People went to bed shortly after sundown ("first sleep"), awoke during the midpoint of the night for an hour or so, then went back to bed ("second sleep") until sunrise. Surprisingly, our consecutive eight-hour period of sleep is a new practice acquired when we transitioned into the industrial age with its subsequent invention of the light bulb.[7]

In keeping with biblical custom, a Christian manual of prayers written in the 1600s included "Directions for Midnight." It instructed people during that waking period to pray and reflect on Scripture.[8] Even in that era, believers expressed the same concerns about nightmares, demons, curses, crime, and misfortune.[9]

Ancient Jews developed several prayers to ward off evils of the night. One of their famous bedtime prayers is called the "Hashkiveinu":[10]

Lie us down to peace, Adonai our God, and raise us up to life, our king (protector), and spread over us the shelter of your peace, and direct us with good advice before You, and

6. As an example of confusion among even literary scholars regarding biphasal sleep, a 1932 English version of *The Odyssey* translates book 4, line 414 as, "When you see him settle down." However, the Greek actually reads, "Wait until his first sleep" ("Why Humans Are Supposed to Sleep in Two 4-Hour Phases," Half as Interesting, August 12, 2021, https://youtube.com/watch?v=DKBXFfEPJyg&si=yOAgtx1ztBrpB9Dd).

7. Roger Ekirch, "Sleep We Have Lost: Pre-Industrial Slumber in the British Isles," *The American Historical Review* 106, no. 2 (April 2001): 344, 366–67, 383.

8. Thomas Ken, *A Manual of Prayers for the Use of the Scholars of Winchester College* (London: John Martyn, 1675).

9. Ekirch, "Sleep We Have Lost," 357.

10. Hebrew: השכיבנו (*hashkiveinu*), "to lie down."

save us for the sake of your name, and look out for us, and keep enemies, plagues, swords, famines, and troubles from our midst, and *remove Satan from in front of us and from behind us*, and cradle us in the shadow of your wings, for You are God who guards us and saves us, for You are God.[11]

Also, they devised other strong night prayers:

Save us . . . from a bad man, from a bad mishap, from an evil instinct, from a bad companion, from a bad neighbor, *from the destructive Satan*, from a harsh trial and from a harsh opponent. . . .[12]

Save me from a bad mishap, from the evil inclination, from a bad woman, and from all evils that suddenly come upon the world. And all who plan evil against me, swiftly thwart their counsel, and frustrate their plans.[13]

However, as I discovered, demonic attacks are not just limited to the night. Jewish literature records the case of two rabbis who were harmed by a demon during the day when they entered a haunted building.[14] Also, it's documented that the "night-demons and morning-demons and midday-demons fled from among" the believers whenever

---

11. "Hashkiveinu," Sefaria, accessed January 18, 2024, https://www.sefaria .org/sheets/29587?lang=bi, emphasis added. See also Hara Person, "Hashkiveinu: Seeking Comfort and Protection through the Night," My Jewish Learning, accessed December 13, 2023, https://www.myjewishlearning.com/article/hash kiveinu-seeking-comfort-and-protection-through-the-night/. Person explains that many modern (rationalist) rabbis shun the ancient Jewish teachings on demons, so the Reform Jewish prayer book omits the phrase about protection from Satan.
12. BT, Berakhot 16b.23, emphasis added.
13. BT, Berakhot 17a.4.
14. BT, Kiddushin 29b.12.

the temple's incense of prayers was lit.[15] In summary, prayer remains the means by which believers seek protection from demons—especially at night.

THE ANCIENT PRAYER THAT ENDED NIGHTMARES AND SLEEP PARALYSIS

When I went off to university, I still experienced periodic nightmares and sleep paralysis. I fasted, prayed, read my Bible—nothing stopped them. I even researched spiritual warfare prayers, but the demons found a way to occasionally bypass those too. I was desperate, and I prayed for relief.

Then one day I was watching Christian TV, and the speaker recommended believers begin a daily practice of reciting the Lord's Prayer. I was skeptical, but what did I have to lose? I recited the Lord's Prayer, went to bed, woke up, sat up, looked around, and said to myself, "Hmmm, let's see if it works again tonight." I recited the prayer the next night—same outcome. I tried it the next night and every night after that for over 30 years—with zero sleep disturbances ever since.

I once taught a Bible study on the Lord's Prayer. As an experiment, I gave the more than 30 students an assignment to recite it at bedtime and come back the next week to share their experience. All of the students confirmed they had no nightmares that week.

One of the attendees was deathly terrified of insects because she had experienced night terrors ever since she was a child. She vividly dreamed of being covered in cockroaches. She would wake up in the middle of the night fighting them off her—scaring her roommate half to death. After she

15. Aramaic Targum to Song of Songs 4.6.

started reciting the Lord's Prayer at bedtime, the night terrors instantly stopped. As if the evil one wanted to make a point, she awoke one morning to find a bug poised on her pillow. She calmly rose out of bed, then did something she never had the courage to do in over 20 years—she killed that insect. Then she went through the apartment complex on a bug-killing campaign. Her roommate and neighbors knew God worked a miracle.

At every military base where I was stationed, I took the liberty to either preach or teach on the Lord's Prayer, and I recommended believers start and end their day with it. I was astonished to receive numerous testimonies that went beyond just relief from nightmares and sleep paralysis. Here are three:

1. A young lady and her husband had divorce papers awaiting signature. She had done everything in her power to save their marriage, to no avail. That Sunday after church, she started reciting the Lord's Prayer. The next day her husband mysteriously decided he no longer wanted the divorce.

2. A senior ranking officer and his wife suffered multiple family tragedies and health challenges. Sadness overwhelmed them. After a few days of reciting the Lord's Prayer, they experienced an overflow of unmatched peace and joy like never before.

3. A retired veteran started a business, and it was all but a bust. On day two of reciting the Lord's Prayer, she obtained a client worth over $250,000 in business income.

The above testimonies validate there are New Covenant benefits to reciting the Lord's Prayer. But why?

UNDERSTANDING ANCIENT PRAYER

Renowned Hebrew scholar Dr. Douglas Stuart warns, "The Bible is such a historically oriented revelation that *ignoring historical context* tends to assure misinterpretation."[16] For example, my church denomination taught that the Lord's Prayer is a sample prayer. However, there's a well-known saying in the science of scriptural interpretation: "A text without a context is a pretext for a proof text." In other words, you can make a Scripture mean anything if you don't consider its historical, linguistic, and literary factors.

As my research will show, there's no way to grasp the significance of the Lord's Prayer without knowing the ancient Jewish practice of prayer, along with analyzing the related biblical languages and how the earliest Christians understood, taught, and applied it.

Ponder this quote from a church manual (first century AD) entitled "The Lord's Teaching through the Twelve Apostles to the Nations":[17]

Neither pray as the hypocrites do, but *as the Lord commanded in his Gospel, thus you are to pray,*[18] "Our Father, who is in Heaven, let Your Name be sanctified; let Your Kingdom come; let Your will be done on earth as it is in Heaven;[19] give us today our daily bread, and forgive us our debt as we forgive our debtors; and lead us not into temptation, but

16. Douglas Stuart, *Old Testament Exegesis* (Philadelphia: Westminster, 1984), 53, emphasis added.
17. The original title is *Didache*, a Greek word meaning "teaching."
18. This verb is rendered in Greek as a present continuous command consistent with Jesus's command in Matt. 6:9–13 and Luke 11:2–4.
19. The literal Greek phrase is "as in Heaven so also on earth."

deliver us from the Evil One; for Yours is the power and the glory forever." *Thus, pray three times a day.*[20]

Christians living in New Testament times recited the Lord's Prayer

1. in place of the Jewish corporate prayer (Amidah);
2. as Jesus taught and commanded them; and
3. three times a day according to biblical custom.

I'll expand on each of these in the sections below.

THE NEW COVENANT "LORD'S PRAYER" REPLACED THE OLD COVENANT "LORD'S PRAYER"

First, here are five facts about the Lord's Prayer replacing the ancient Amidah:

1. The Amidah[21] is the Old Covenant corporate prayer recited in the plural ("us," "our").[22]
2. It is the Old Covenant "Lord's Prayer," because the literal Hebrew rendering of Isaiah 56:7 refers to the temple as "the house of *my* prayer."[23]

---

20. Didache 8:2–3, author's translation from Greek, emphasis added.
21. Hebrew for "standing"; thus, the prayer is offered while standing.
22. The Amidah is believed to have been formulated in the fourth century BC. Per discussions with Jewish military chaplains, this date is traced back to the Great Assembly led by Nehemiah (governor) and Ezra (a priest and scribe), who facilitated the return of the exiles to Jerusalem. However, some rabbis trace the origins of the Amidah further back to the time of Daniel. This corporate prayer became vitally important when they could not present the daily whole burnt offerings due to Babylonian captivity and the destruction of the first temple.
23. In Hebrew, the wording is not "my house of prayer" but "the house of my prayer."

3. It is also referred to as "The Prayer" (*HaTephillah* in Hebrew):[24]

    a. it stems from a Hebrew verb root meaning "to self-judge";

    b. thus, during prayer, we evaluate our commitment to God.

4. It includes "sanctifying the name" (*Kiddush HaShem* in Hebrew):[25]

    a. it is based on Leviticus 22:31–32: "So you shall keep my commandments. . . . You shall not profane my holy name, that I may be sanctified among the people of Israel. I am the LORD who sanctifies you";

    b. by obeying God, believers exhibit behavior consistent with the holiness of His Name.

5. *Now*, the prayer God the Son taught us (Matt. 6:9; Luke 11:2):

    a. is the New Covenant "Lord's Prayer" recited in the corporate plural ("us," "our");

    b. is "The Prayer"—used 26 times in the Greek New Testament;[26] in 16 places, it is listed in conjunction with

---

24. Hebrew: תפילה (*tefillah*), "prayer." The root פלל (*palal*) means "to judge" (Exod. 21:22; Deut. 32:31; Job 31:11). Thus, prayer is self-evaluation. See also Eliyahu Lizorkin-Eyzenberg, "What Does Prayer Mean in Hebrew?," Israel Bible Center, March 1, 2021, https://weekly.israelbiblecenter.com/prayer-mean-hebrew#:~:text=The%20Jewish%20concept%20of%20prayer,is%20self%2Djudgement%20or%20introspection.

25. The *Kiddush HaShem* (קידוש השם—"sanctification of the name") is an ancient Hebrew phrase that should result in holy behavior that doesn't dishonor God (Lev. 22:31–32). See also Maimonides, Yesoday Hatorah 5.1, 11.

26. The noun form of προσευχῇ (prayer) is used 36 times in the New Testament. Twenty-six times it's used with the article "the" (τῇ προσευχῇ), denoting a specific prayer (Matt. 21:22; Luke 6:12; 22:45; Acts 1:14; 2:42; 3:1; 6:4; 10:4,

    i. the period of evening *corporate* prayer (Luke 6:12; 22:45; Acts 1:14);

    ii. the ninth hour of the *corporate* whole offering (Acts 3:1; 10:30–31);

    iii. the daily lighting of the *corporate* incense of prayer (Rev. 5:8; 8:3–4);[27]

    iv. the four *corporate* actions of Christian discipleship (Acts 2:42; 16:16a);

    v. the *corporate* prayer distinct from the "petitions" and "thanksgiving" segments (Eph. 1:16; Phil. 4:6; Col. 4:2; 1 Thess. 1:2; 1 Tim. 5:5; Philem. 1:4);

  c. maintains the Hebrew custom of *Kiddush HaShem* ("sanctifying the name"):

    i. its first words are "Let Your name be sanctified";[28]

    ii. it is reinforced by the Apostle Peter, who quotes Leviticus 19:2: "As obedient children . . . as he

---

31; 16:16; Rom. 1:10; 12:12; 15:30; 1 Cor. 7:5; Eph. 1:16; Phil. 4:6; Col. 4:2, 12; 1 Thess. 1:2; 1 Tim. 5:5; Philem. 1:4, 22; 1 Pet. 3:7; Rev. 5:8; 8:3, 4). It is reasonable to conclude that Christians began to recite the Lord's Prayer in place of the Amidah, since (1) Jesus commands it [Greek present active imperative], and (2) the Didache confirms it as a command. Also, "the prayer" is distinguished from τῇ δεήσει (the petition). Additionally, I clarify Heb. 5:7 because it is not clear in the English translations: "While Jesus was here on earth, he offered petition (δέησις) and pleadings (ἱκετηρία), with a loud cry and tears, to the one who could rescue him from death." The Greek word (ἱκετηρία) is best translated as "pleas." Besides here, the form is found only one other place, in the Deuterocanonicals (2 Macc. 9:18), where (like here) it refers to Antiochus pleading with God: "When his sufferings did not in any way diminish, for the judgment of God had justly come upon him, he gave up all hope for himself and wrote to the Jews the following letter, in the form of a plea."

27. These events are heavenly realities of which the temple was a replica. At evening and morning, the priest lit the incense that served as a fragrant symbol of corporate prayer (Exod. 30:7–8).

28. Most English translations have "Hallowed be Your name." However, the literal Greek is consistent with the Hebrew, "Let Your name be sanctified."

who called you is holy, you also be holy in all your conduct, since it is written, 'You shall be holy, for I am holy'" (1 Pet. 1:14–16);

iii. it re-emphasizes that, by obeying God, believers exhibit behavior consistent with the holiness of His Name.

THE LORD'S PRAYER RECOGNIZED AS A COMMAND

Second, here are four facts validating the Lord's Prayer as a command:

1. The Greek language renders the Lord's Prayer as a continuous command,[29] indicating Jesus intended us to recite it every day.

2. Coincidentally, the Amidah was structured into three parts: praise, petitions, and thanksgiving:[30]

   a. praise preceded petitions—it was taught that a believer should approach God, first, with adoration and then, second, with requests—as Moses exemplified (Deut. 3:23–25);[31]

---

29. Matt. 6:9 and Luke 11:2 render Jesus's instruction of the Lord's Prayer in the Greek verb structure of the present active imperative, meaning a continuous command. It has the *exact* verbal construction as the commands Jesus gives us to love our enemies and pray for our persecutors (Matt. 5:41–44).

30. See Daniel Kohn's "The Amidah" (https://www.myjewishlearning.com/article/the-amidah/). It's divided into three sections: Praise (blessings 1–3 relate to foundational beliefs about God), Petitions (blessings 4–16 relate to individual and national needs), and Thanksgiving (blessings 17–19 relate to service and gratitude to God). As he states, "The total number of blessings recited was 18, hence, an early synonym for the Amidah was the Shemonah Esrei, or the Eighteen. However, in Rabbinic times, another blessing was added resulting in a total of 19, yet the original name of the Shemonah Esrei was retained."

31. BT, Berakhot 32a.32.

    b. thanksgiving was the appropriate ending to prayer; also, it was to be a way of life—believers were taught to thank God for at least 100 things per day.[32]

3. Likewise, the New Covenant "Lord's Prayer" is structured into the *same* three ancient parts: praise, petitions, and thanksgiving (see table below).

4. Likewise, the Apostle Paul commands us to pray using the same three-part structure:

> Be anxious for nothing, but in everything by *the prayer* [the Lord's Prayer] and by *the petition* [segment of the Lord's Prayer listing requests] *with thanksgiving* [segment expressing gratitude], let your requests continue to be made[33] known to God. (Phil. 4:6, author's translation from Greek)[34]

    a. still, praise precedes petitions;

    b. still, thanksgiving is a way of life for believers;

        i. we're commanded to give God thanks in everything we do (Col. 3:17);

---

32. BT, Menachot 43b.15. Also see A. J. Jacobs, "Why Thankfulness and Gratitude Are Jewish Emotions," *Forward*, November 20, 2018, https://forward.com /culture/414468/why-thankfulness-and-gratitude-are-jewish-emotions/. He quotes a rabbi who taught that the term *Jew* comes from *Judah* (*Yehudah* in Hebrew), meaning "thanksgiving." However, the origin is also debated. See Elon Gilad, "Why Are Jews Called Jews?," *Haaretz*, February 15, 2017, https://www.haaretz .com/archaeology/2017-02-15/ty-article/why-are-jews-called-jews/0000017f-dbeb -d856-a37f-ffeb3f760000.

33. This Greek verb structure is present passive imperative (continuous command).

34. As mentioned earlier, the Greek's use of the article implies a specific singular prayer and a specific singular segment for petitions, with the prayer period ending with thanksgiving. All are consistent with the ancient Jewish pattern of prayer. This is also demonstrated in the Amidah that was replaced by the New Covenant Lord's Prayer.

ii. consistent with Jewish custom, early Christians ended the Lord's Prayer with "Yours is the kingdom, power, and glory forever"— similar to the gratitude expressed by King David (1 Chron. 29:10–13).

THE LORD'S PRAYER WAS RECITED THREE TIMES A DAY

Third and finally, the Lord's Prayer not only replaced the Amidah and was understood to be a command but also was recited three times a day. Here are two more facts:

1. Ancient Jews recited the Amidah three times a day—the reason is debated,[35] but here are a few explanations:

   a. as a corporate prayer, it became linked to the corporate whole burnt offering;[36]

   b. because David prayed at morning, midday, and evening (Ps. 55:17);[37]

   c. because Daniel prayed three times a day (Dan. 6:10).[38]

---

35. BT, Berakhot 26b.4–10. While ancient sages couldn't conclude the origin of this spiritual practice, we should take heed of the fact that they deemed it essential to the believer's well-being.

36. It was offered twice a day at the Jewish third hour (approximately 9 a.m. or three hours after sunrise) and ninth hour (approximately 3 p.m. or three hours before sundown). The third period of prayer was added in conjunction with the burning of the limbs from the last offering that goes through the night (Yehuda Shurpin, "Why Do Jews Pray Three Times a Day?," Chabad.org, accessed March 20, 2024, http://www.chabad.org/library/article_cdo/aid/3169553/jewish/Why-Do-Jews-Pray-Three-Times-a-Day.htm).

37. BT, Berakhot 31a.23.

38. BT, Berakhot 31a.20.

2. Likewise, Jesus, the Apostle Peter, and early Christians maintained this custom:

   a. Jesus is recorded praying in the morning (Mark 1:35), evening (Matt. 14:23), and seemingly midday (Luke 11:1)[39];

   b. Peter is recorded on three occasions praying during the whole offering periods (Acts 2:1–4; 3:1; 10:9);

   c. again, early Christians taught believers to pray three times a day,[40] and historical records verify Christians reciting the Lord's Prayer for over 1,700 years.[41]

UNDERSTANDING THE LORD'S PRAYER

This naturally leads us to the final section before I conclude. Now that we have explored the historical and biblical contexts related to prayer, I believe we can grasp the significance of the Lord's Prayer. God the Son displayed His genius when He created this theological masterpiece. The table below is my effort to help us understand it.

---

39. The Bible lists in two places where Jesus taught His prayer (Matt. 5:1, starting with the Sermon on the Mount, and Luke 11:1). If Luke speaks of the same occasion as Matthew, then the time period would indicate Jesus prayed and taught around midday. Nevertheless, we at least see examples of Jesus praying in the morning and evening.

40. Didache 8:2–3.

41. Michael G. Brown, "Why Pray the Lord's Prayer?," *The Banner of Truth* (2007), accessed January 18, 2024, https://www.christianstudylibrary.org/article /why-pray-lord%E2%80%99s-prayer. He notes, "In all of the liturgies of the Reformation, including those drafted by Martin Bucer (1539), John Calvin (1542), Thomas Cranmer (1552), John Knox (1556), and others, the practice of praying the Lord's Prayer was included as a regular part of public worship."

Jesus commands, "Seek first His kingdom and His righteousness, and all these [earthly] things will be added to you" (Matt. 6:33 NASB).

R E C O M M I T M E N T	Submission through Praise[42]	First, Seek
	1. Let Your Name be sanctified.[43]	Holiness
	2. Let Your kingdom come.	Allegiance
	3. Let Your will be done on earth as it is in heaven.	Obedience
	Dependence through Petition	Second, Ask
	1. Give us this day our daily bread.	Provision
	2. Forgive us our debts as we forgive our debtors.[44]	Pardon
	3. Lead us not into temptation but deliver us from the evil one.	Protection

Here are three takeaways from the Lord's Prayer:

1. We recommit ourselves to God by expressing our submission to and dependence on Him, in His own words;

    a. submission is expressed through praise:

        i. by committing to holiness, allegiance, and obedience;

        ii. those three heavenly priorities satisfy God by reinforcing a lifestyle of repentance;

42. The words *let us* validate submission to God in that (1) His Name is already holy and cannot be changed (Mal. 3:6); (2) His kingdom advances and cannot be stopped (Isa. 45:23; Rom. 14:11); and (3) His will shall be accomplished and cannot fail (Luke 1:37). Thus, we submit to these unalterable realities when we recite this prayer.

43. Again, this is the literal Greek rendering. It is traced to the ancient Hebrew phrase known as the *Kiddush HaShem* (קידוש השם), "sanctification of the name." The biblical outgrowth is holy behavior: "You must faithfully keep all my commands. . . . Do not bring shame on my holy name. . . . I am the LORD who makes you holy" (Lev. 22:31–32 NLT).

44. Debt is a perfect biblical metaphor for sin. When someone sins against us, we naturally respond with "You owe me" or "I owe you." The ultimate goal of forgiveness is choosing not to retaliate by repaying evil for evil.

    b. dependence is expressed through petitions:

        i. by relying on God for provision, pardon, and protection;

        ii. those three earthly concerns satisfy us by covering all general areas of human need.

2. It is short, for God declares, "Before they call I will answer; while they are yet speaking I will hear" (Isa. 65:24).

3. It is corporate rather than individual ("us," "our")—we recite it as a member of the body of Christ (a part of the whole), for "if one member suffers, all suffer together; if one member is honored, all rejoice together" (1 Cor. 12:26).

When my wife and I were teaching our children how to pray, we set the tone by asking everyone to share something for which they were thankful. Next, we recited the Lord's Prayer together. Afterward, we paused to allow for any individual petitions—specific ways we desired God to provide for, pardon, or protect us or someone else.

Over the years, I don't recall our children experiencing any abnormal sleep disturbances—unless they went to bed afraid from sneaking to watch *Scooby Doo*. Also, the Bible reminds us that worry can be a source of bad dreams too: "A dream comes when there are many cares" (Eccles. 5:3 NIV). On such occasions, we must remember to petition God regarding our specific needs.

Since protection from Satan is one of the petitions in the Lord's Prayer, Dr. C. Fred Dickason reminds us, "Believers would do well to *obey* Christ and pray this prayer daily. . . .

Why did the Lord teach that this was a *necessary* prayer? Is there some danger involved? It seems there is."[45]

SURROUNDED BY ANCIENT EVIL—BUT PROTECTED BY "THE PRAYER"

I usually complete my research and writing in my home office. However, one evening my wife asked me to bring my laptop to the bedroom so we could at least be in the same room. Unfortunately, I had been working long hours all week due to finalizing one of the chapters. I was fascinated by an ancient exorcism prayer I found, so I downloaded it and ended the night with my feet propped up in the bed reading it.

That night, I had a bizarre dream. I saw my wife and myself fast asleep and surrounded by numerous demonic spirits. They were standing on each side of us, leaning over, and peering in like they were curious. To my surprise, they all looked different—various sizes, shapes, and colors. One was bright—reminding me of the Bible's warning, "Satan disguises himself as an angel of light" (2 Cor. 11:14 NLT).

The one that was most active was a werewolf-like creature about seven feet tall. He was pitch-black—darker than any black I have ever seen. He kept pacing around the bed— even walking through the wall behind the headboard. His movements indicated he wanted to pounce on us but was prevented by some type of invisible shield around us.

The next morning, I woke up and said, "Wow, I need to lay off some of my late-night research." I could relate to the Roman governor Festus when he told the Apostle Paul, "Too much study has made you crazy!" (Acts 26:24 NLT).

45. C. Fred Dickason, *Demon Possession & the Christian* (Wheaton: Crossway, 1987), 90, emphasis added.

To my shock, a couple of days later, I coincidentally found two historical sources related to evil spirits. The first was from ancient literature: "A demon changes into different forms and colors."[46] The second was from an archaeological discovery: "This [prayer is] to bind, and muzzle, and lock up, and take out, and remove all demons, and dews, and *howlers*, and lilis [sexual demons], and tormentors, and evil spirits. . . . Go out and remove yourselves."[47]

Those centuries-old records described the same spirits I saw! I believe that exorcism prayer I read caught their attention. Yet God providentially allowed me a glimpse into the unseen realm to see that although those demons were present, they could *not* harm us, because we were protected by the Lord's Prayer.

---

46. BT, Yoma 75a.

47. Discovered during an archaeological dig, this is part of a binding prayer from a Jewish incantation bowl used to ward off demons. See Dan Levene, *A Corpus of Magic Bowls: Incantation Texts in Jewish Aramaic from Late Antiquity* (London: Kegan Paul, 2003), emphasis added.

PART 2

BIBLICAL INSIGHTS

16 TRUE STORIES

4

THE ORIGIN OF DEMONS

In the first three chapters, I shared my *personal encounters* with evil spirits. Now we embark upon a new section of the book where we examine *biblical insights* into demons and demonization.

In this chapter, I focus on six important points from biblical history on the subject of demons:

1. The Biblically Incomplete Origin of Demons;
2. Evil Angels, Rulers, Authorities, and Powers;
3. Angelic Rebellion #1—A Power-Hungry "Watcher";
4. Angelic Rebellion #2—Sex-Craving Angels;
5. More Rebellion—Fame-Seeking Humans; and
6. Humanity's Plight but God's Rescue.

THE BIBLICALLY INCOMPLETE ORIGIN OF DEMONS

As we strive to dispel the darkness with the light of Christ, who are we exposing? The Bible declares, "Our wrestling-match is not against flesh and blood but against the rulers, against the authorities, against the world-powers of this dark-realm,[1] against the spiritual evil in the heavenly places" (Eph. 6:12, author's translation from Greek). In other words, we're in hand-to-hand combat[2] against spiritual forces with superior abilities who are evil, nonhuman, and not from this world. What is the origin of such beings?

Surprisingly, the Bible doesn't tell us the exact origin of demons. We do read in the Old Testament of rebellious angels and how they influenced sinful activities like murder (Gen. 4:4–8),[3] false worship (Deut. 32:16–17), and unjust wars (1 Kings 22:20–22). However, this whole section of the Bible is vague on the origin of demons.

This uncertainty caused even ancient Jewish believers to speculate.[4] Interestingly, some modern scholars and pastors appeal to a belief from the Second Temple period (515 BC to AD 70).[5] It taught that demons are the spirits of dead Nephilim (giants) fathered by the fallen angels and the women they took (Gen. 6:2–4).[6] However, that viewpoint did

1. The Friberg's Greek Lexicon offers these translations for:
   a. entry 16491, κοσμοκράτωρ (*kosmokratōr*), "world-power"—one holding power over the world; spirit-beings who control parts of the world system; and
   b. entry 24626, σκότος (*skotos*), "darkness"—literally an enveloping sphere where light is absent; also metaphorically, as the domain under the authority of the devil and demons, realm of evil, evil world.
2. The "hand-to-hand combat" analogy is derived from the "sword of the Spirit" metaphor based on the Greek word μάχαιρα (*machaira*), "small sword or dagger." It is a weapon for close combat (Friberg, 17892).
3. Compared to 1 John 3:12: "We should not be like Cain, who was of the evil one and murdered his brother."
4. Gideon Bohak, "Conceptualizing Demons in Late Jewish Antique Judaism," in *Demons and Illness from Antiquity to the Early-Modern Period*, ed. Siam Bhayro and Catherine Rider (Leiden, the Netherlands: Brill, 2017), 128.
5. Michael S. Heiser, *Demons* (Bellingham, WA: Lexham Press, 2020), 241–42.
6. From nonbiblical 1 Enoch 15:8–10. It's important to note that ancient Jews didn't consider the Books of Enoch divinely inspired because they're written

not persist with ancient rabbis who discussed many ideas on the origin of demons.[7] Yet as Dr. Gideon Bohak, a professor of Jewish philosophy at Tel Aviv University, explains further, "The different explanations did not necessarily compete with each other, since the presence of many different types of demons probably called for more than one explanation of their origins."[8]

Thankfully, the New Testament removes a lot of ambiguity by simply defining demons as "the devil and his angels" (Matt. 25:41; Rev. 12:7). Also, it elaborates on other aspects. For instance, in Revelation 12:9, we discover the "serpent" that deceived Eve (Gen. 3:1) was in fact "the great dragon . . . that ancient serpent, who is called the devil and Satan, the deceiver of the whole world."

While the New Testament specifies certain aspects about demons, it still doesn't tell us the complete story. For example, we're never told the specific origin of the 200 million demons to be released in the end times (Rev. 9:16). Moreover,

---

in Greek, not Hebrew. Also, along with early Christians, they referred to these books as pseudepigrapha—writings falsely attributed to an author—especially since Enoch lived 365 years in the pre-flood era (Gen. 5:23–24). Nevertheless, these books were found along with biblical Scriptures during the archaeological discovery of the Dead Sea Scrolls. This validated their ancient influence. However, the New Testament teaches evil spirits are comprised of "the devil and his angels" (Matt. 25:41; see Rev. 12:7–9). If one is adamant about aligning their view with the Second Temple belief that Nephilim became demons after death, then this category *could* technically apply to them too, since they are angel-human hybrids.

7. See Bohak, "Conceptualizing Demons in Late Antique Judaism," 128. Dr. Bohak lists a few *more* rabbinic explanations in addition to the dead Nephilim view: (1) the souls of evil people (Josephus, *War* 7.185); (2) humans left unfinished due to the start of the Sabbath (Avot 5:6); (3) offspring from the union of Adam and Lilith during his abstinence from Eve after the Fall (Eruv 18b); and (4) other beliefs including the claim that God turned some of the builders of the Tower of Babel into demons (Sanhedrin 109a).

8. Bohak, "Conceptualizing Demons in Late Antique Judaism," 128.

scholars debate a later belief that Satan convinced one-third of the angels to join him in his rebellion (12:4). One reason is because the symbolic event—the dragon sweeping away one-third of the stars—is in the same verse with the birth of Christ.[9] Thus, Satan's war in heaven seems to be a chronological account within New Testament times describing a demonic protest in response to the atoning work of Christ.

Nevertheless, since the subject of evil began in the Old Testament, we must start there for an overall understanding.

EVIL ANGELS, RULERS, AUTHORITIES, AND POWERS

Earlier, we read where the New Testament refers to demons as *evil* angels, rulers, authorities, and powers. From what are these titles derived? We find our answers in the Old Testament.

9. Consider the thoughts of these three scholars:
   a. Gregory K. Beale, *The Book of Revelation* (Grand Rapids: Eerdmans, 1999), 637: "The tail of the dragon here is afflicting people and not merely or primarily angels. . . . Perhaps the falling stars . . . represent deceived Israel, who falls away and was never truly identified with the stars of Rev. 12:1."
   b. George E. Ladd, *Revelation of John* (Grand Rapids: Eerdmans, 1972), 169: "There is no need to see in these words anything more than the fearful appearance of this monster. . . . The dragon is such a colossal creature that with one sweep of his tail he can brush a third of the stars out of their natural position."
   c. Heiser, *Demons*, 243–45: "This is an excellent example of how a Christian tradition can become doctrine. There isn't a single verse in the entirety of Scripture that tells us (a) the original rebel sinned before the episode of Genesis 3, or (b) a third of the angels also fell either before humanity's fall or at the time of the fall. There is only one passage that mentions a 'third' of the angels (presumably) and Satan/the serpent in tandem (Rev. 12:1–9). . . . Since there is no other passage in the Bible that uses the 'third' language in conjunction with a satanic conflict, the idea that Satan and one-third of the angels rebelled at that time is a traditional myth."

First, we must analyze the terms *morning stars* and *sons of God*. In Job 38:7, God uses them to refer to the spiritual beings who sang and rejoiced while He created the heavens and the earth. Most scholars believe these titles describe the same beings.[10] In other words, "morning star" describes the radiance of these "sons of God."[11]

What is meant by "sons of God"? The Hebrew word for "God" in this phrase is *Elohim*.[12] In this case, it is used in the general sense to refer to supernatural beings.[13] For further clarity, when ancient scribes translated the Hebrew Scriptures into the Greek Septuagint (around 300 BC), they rendered "sons of God" in Job 38:7 as "all my angels."[14] Therefore, they understood these beings to be God's angels.

Second, these specific angels also comprise the "divine council." They serve in God's royal court and assist Him

10. This is known as synonymous parallelism where the Scripture is speaking poetically.

11. This is a common biblical description of godly beings who radiate God's likeness. We also find examples in the New Testament. On one occasion, Jesus allows three of His disciples to see His true nature: "And he was transfigured before them, and his face shone like the sun, and his clothes became white as light" (Matt. 17:2; see also 2 Pet. 1:19; Rev. 2:28; 22:16).

12. The context determines if it is translated as either "God" or "gods." This is why the Old Testament occasionally adds a title before it to differentiate between "gods" and "the God"—for example, "Elyon Elohim" (Most High God). See also Ps. 78:35, 56; Dan. 3:26; 4:2; 5:18, 21.

13. In Hebrew, Gen. 35:7 uses *elohim* in the plural, although translations almost always render it in the singular. The English version reads, "There he [Jacob] built an altar, and he called the place El Bethel, because it was there that *God revealed himself* to him when he was fleeing from his brother" (NIV). However, it actually reads in Hebrew, "*Elohim* revealed themselves," referring back to Jacob's vision of God and angels (Gen. 28:12). Additionally, the Witch of Endor mistakes the spirit of Saul for an *elohim* (1 Sam. 28:13).

14. The scribes did the same for Job 1:6; 2:1; see also Deut. 32:8, 43; Pss. 8:5; 97:7; 138:1.

in human affairs. Additionally, they surround God's throne on lesser thrones:

> As I looked,
>
>> thrones [plural] were set in place,
>>> and the Ancient of Days [God] took his seat. . . .
>> His throne [singular] was flaming with fire,
>>> and its wheels were all ablaze. . . .
>> Thousands upon thousands [of angels] attended him;
>>> ten thousand times ten thousand stood before
>>>> him.
>> The court was seated,
>>> and the books were opened. (Dan. 7:9–10 NIV)

Moreover, Daniel refers to members of God's divine council as "watchers" (Dan. 4:13). This term further specifies their duties of monitoring humans and enforcing decrees on behalf of God (v. 17).[15]

As shown above, the titles "morning star," "sons of God," "watchers," and "divine council" describe a group of angels who are granted thrones subordinate to God's and are delegated responsibilities over human affairs. In essence, they are spiritual beings with superior abilities who are nonhuman and not from this world. Do these words sound familiar? They're from the same description above of Satan and his angels—except, they're not determined to be *evil*, yet.

---

15. Ancient theologians saw the need to clarify the authority of the watchers: "Why do I need these instances of plural [thrones]? Why does [Dan. 7:9] employ the plural at all when referring to God? . . . The Holy One, blessed be He, does not act unless He consults with the [divine council], as it is stated: 'The matter is by the decree of the watchers, and the sentence by the word of the holy ones' [Dan. 4:17]" (BT, Sanhedrin 38b.16).

ANGELIC REBELLION #1—A POWER-HUNGRY "WATCHER"

The Bible describes the first angelic rebellion in Isaiah 14:12–14. God speaks to the rogue spiritual being influencing the King of Babylon:

> How you have fallen from Heaven, Shining One, Son
>   of the Morning.
> You were cut down [falling] to the earth weakening[16]
>   the nations.
> You said inwardly:
> I will ascend to heaven,
> I will exalt my throne far above the stars of God, and
> I will sit upon the mount of assembly in the highest
>   part of the north.
> I will ascend above the tops of the clouds.
> I will be like the Most High. (author's translation
>   from Hebrew)

Consider these two facts: (1) this nonhuman being fell from heaven, and (2) the titles "shining one" and "son of the morning" are like the ones used in Job 38:7 to describe the angels referred to as the watchers of the divine council. When the Hebrew word for "shining one"[17] is translated

---

16. Hebrew: חלש (*khaw-lash*) can also mean "to prostrate" or "to destroy," per Francis Brown, S. R. Driver, and Charles A. Briggs, *Hebrew-Aramaic and English Lexicon of the Old Testament* (abridged BDB-Gesenius Lexicon) (Ontario: Online Bible Foundation, 1997), entry 3135; hereafter BDB. It is used in Exod. 17:13 when Joshua makes the Amalekites "bow down" to the "mouth of the sword" (literal Hebrew). It is also used to refer to ability: "Let the weak [*khaw-lash*] say, 'I am strong!'" (Joel 3:10 NKJV).

17. Hebrew: הילל (*helel*), "morning star" (also "shining one"), per William L. Holladay, *A Concise Hebrew and Aramaic Lexicon of the Old Testament* (Leiden, the Netherlands: Brill, 2000), entry 2001; hereafter Holladay.

into Latin, it becomes "Lucifer," meaning "light-bearer."[18] It was the original name in Latin for the planet Venus— the brightest planet that can be seen before sunrise (thus, the "morning star"). So the Prophet Isaiah is describing the fall of Satan[19]—a former watcher plus expelled member of the divine council. Jesus validates this when teaching about casting out demons: "I saw Satan fall like lightning from heaven" (Luke 10:18).

How did Satan become evil? His five "I will" statements indicate it was pride. Likewise, the church is warned not to appoint unproven leaders, because they "may become conceited and fall under the same judgment as the devil" (1 Tim. 3:6 NIV). Also, in the phrase "I will exalt my throne *above* the stars of God" (Isa. 14:13 NKJV), the Hebrew word translated "above"[20] indicates Satan's sinister intentions. He wasn't satisfied with his heavenly position. As the results of his actions prove, he sought to be "like God in control, not in character."[21]

Stunningly, Satan never voiced his thoughts—God knew them and judged him accordingly. It appears He thwarted Satan's plans before he could fully act on them. This will be confirmed again by the phrase "iniquity was found in you" (Ezek. 28:15 RSV). This is why God warns us, "I the LORD search the heart and examine the mind, to reward each

18. Translators of the King James Version relied on the Latin Vulgate as a source.

19. In the Old Testament, "satan" is not an official name—it appears as "the satan," meaning "the adversary" (Job 1:8–12; 2:3–7; Zech. 3:1). It is not until the New Testament period that "Satan" becomes historically clarified to be the title of the chief demon.

20. Hebrew: מעל (*maal*) also indicates an unfaithful or treacherous act (BDB, 5506).

21. Dickason, *Demon Possession & the Christian*, 63.

person according to their conduct, according to what their deeds deserve" (Jer. 17:10 NIV).

Additionally, Satan's plan to "ascend to heaven" indicates his rebellion possibly occurred while attending to his duties on earth. Due to this, God permanently banished him there. This may be when he doubled down in bitterness and tempted Eve with the same desires that led to his own fall. As the Prophet Isaiah declared, Satan's exile to earth led to the moral weakness of the world (Isa. 14:12).

God speaks again to Satan, since he's the evil spirit also influencing the King of Tyre:

> You were in Eden, the garden of God;
> Every precious stone was your covering. . . .
> The workmanship of your timbrels and pipes
> Was prepared for you on the day you were created.
>
> You were the anointed cherub who covers;
> I established you;
> You were on the holy mountain of God;
> You walked back and forth in the midst of fiery stones.
> You were perfect in your ways from the day you were
>   created,
> Till *iniquity* was found in you. (Ezek. 28:13–15 NKJV)

Observe these four subpoints about Satan:

1. he was appointed as a guardian angel ("cherub") described as a creature with wings plus human and animal-like features (Ezek. 1:5–11);
2. he had specific duties in the garden of Eden;

3. he was faultless but later yielded to evil desires; and

4. he had free access to God's royal court—until he was
   banished to earth; his visits were limited to accusations against humans until he protested the atonement and was permanently banned.[22]

Interestingly, we can obtain more details about Satan's appearance before his fall. As we analyze other Scriptures, it appears that angels rotated duties, because in the Prophet Ezekiel's vision, he saw cherubim (plural) around God's throne. However, the Prophet Isaiah saw seraphim (plural; the singular is "seraph"):

> I saw the Lord, high and exalted, seated on a throne. . . .
> Above him were seraphim, each with six wings: With two
> wings they covered their faces, with two they covered their
> feet, and with two they were flying. And they were calling
> to one another: "Holy, holy, holy is the LORD Almighty; the
> whole earth is full of his glory." (Isa. 6:1–3 NIV)

The seraphim (like the cherubim) have wings and animal-like features.[23] While no other meaning is given for the Hebrew title "cherub," the word "seraph" (singular) means "fiery serpent."[24] Thus, Satan in his original form was a ra-

---

22. See Job 1:6–7 and 2:1–2 compared to 1 Pet. 5:8; plus Zech. 3:1 compared to Rev. 12:7–10.

23. See Jeffrey J. Niehaus, *Biblical Theology*, vol. 2 (Bellingham, WA: Lexham Press, 2018), 380. He discusses the "living creatures" in Rev. 4:7–8 as being seraphim and not cherubim. Like the seraphim in Isa. 6:1–3, they (1) repeat the same words; (2) have one face, not four like the cherubim (Ezek. 1:10); and (3) have six wings, not four like the cherubim (1:11).

24. Per Holladay (entry 8290), *seraph* means "burning." It comes from the root *saraph*, "to burn," so the nuance of "seraph" as "serpent" means "fiery" (or

diant, winged, snake-like being. This is why the New Testament refers to him as the "ancient serpent called the devil" (Rev. 12:9 NIV). Also, he apparently had legs, since two of his wings covered his feet. Therefore, God further humiliated Satan when He punished him to crawl on his belly. Metaphorically, Satan in his fallen form has clipped wings and amputated legs.

ANGELIC REBELLION #2—SEX-CRAVING ANGELS

If you think the fall of Satan was surprising, this second angelic rebellion is one of the most bizarre cases in all of Scripture. After the Fall of humans and before the great flood, Genesis 6 shocks us:

> When man began to multiply on the face of the land and daughters were born to them, the sons of God saw that the daughters of man were attractive. And they took as their wives any they chose. . . . The Nephilim were on the earth in those days, and also afterward, when the sons of God came into the daughters of man and they bore children to them. These were the mighty men who were of old, the men of renown. The LORD saw that the wickedness of man was great in the earth, and that every intention of the thoughts of his heart was only evil continually. And the LORD regretted that he had made man on the earth, and it grieved him to his heart. So the LORD said, "I will blot out man whom

poisonous) "serpent." For instance, the Prophet Isaiah warns a king in Philistia, "Do not rejoice . . . that the king who attacked you is dead. For from that snake [*seraph*] a more poisonous snake [*nahash*] will be born, a fiery serpent [*seraph*] to destroy you!" (Isa. 14:29 NLT). Additionally, the second word for "snake" (*nahash*) is used in Gen. 3:1 to refer to the snake who deceived Eve.

I have created from the face of the land, man and animals and creeping things and birds of the heavens, for I am sorry that I have made them." But Noah found favor in the eyes of the LORD. (vv. 1–2, 4–8)

The "sons of God" in this passage are the same angels referred to earlier. In fact, this Hebrew phrase is never used in the Old Testament to describe humans. This historical understanding was consistent with ancient Jews and early Christians for nearly 1,000 years.[25] Even the New Testament writers verify:

> For if God did not spare angels when they sinned, but cast them into hell and committed them to chains of gloomy darkness to be kept until the judgment; if he did not spare the ancient world, but preserved Noah, a herald of righteousness, with seven others, when he brought a flood upon the world of the ungodly. (2 Pet. 2:4–5)

> And the angels who did not keep their positions of authority but abandoned their proper dwelling—these he has kept in darkness, bound with everlasting chains for judgment on the great Day. (Jude 6 NIV)

Therefore, the earliest and most long-standing biblical view is that some of the watchers violated angelic protocols by "taking"[26] women and having sex with them. How were they able to do so? Well, in the Bible when angels visit

---

25. See Justin Martyr (*Second Apology* chap. 5 from c. AD 155–60) and Athenagoras (*Plea for the Christians* chap. 25 from c. AD 176–77). This includes Second Temple era ancient Jewish beliefs (515 BC).

26. Hebrew: לקח, *laqach*, "took," translated by some versions as "marry," can also be used to convey rape (i.e., Gen. 34:2) (BDB, 4939).

humans, they look like people.[27] Even in the New Testament we are told, "Do not neglect to show hospitality to strangers, for thereby some have entertained angels unawares" (Heb. 13:2). If angels can appear in human form, eat, and drink (Gen. 18:1–8), then we can conclude they had all the parts of a human body. This is what makes this second angelic rebellion so perverse.

The incident becomes more intriguing. Who are the Nephilim?[28] The ancient Jews understood them to be giants— a race of abnormally tall humans who were great warriors with unmatched physical abilities. This view is confirmed by the title found in only one other verse: "We saw the Nephilim (the sons of Anak, who come from the Nephilim), and we seemed to ourselves like grasshoppers, and so we seemed to them" (Num. 13:33). Also, when the ancient scribes translated the Hebrew Bible into the Greek Septuagint, they used the word "giant" in place of "Nephilim." Although the Bible lists the term in only two places, the topic of giants was consistently discussed in the ancient world—including the story of Goliath, the giant killed by David (1 Sam. 17:4, 43, 49).

What was the origin of the giants? Ancient Jews during the Second Temple period interpreted Genesis 6:4 as a

27. See Gen. 18:1–2, 8–13, 22; 19:1–5; Josh. 5:13–15. In two of these verses, God takes on human form and is accompanied by other angels. The Old Testament signifies this by the phrase "Angel of the Lord." Additionally, the Angel of the Lord is worshiped—an act forbidden for holy angels: "*I fell down to worship at the feet of the angel* . . . but he said to me, '*You must not do that!* I am a fellow servant with you and your brothers the prophets, and with those who keep the words of this book. *Worship God*'" (Rev. 22:8–9).

28. This Hebrew title is used in two places (Gen. 6:4; Num. 13:33) but remains undefined due to debates among scholars. However, the verb form means "to fall" and is translated into various English words (Josh. 8:25; Judg. 20:46; 2 Kings 25:11; Ps. 145:14; Jer. 39:9; 52:15; Ezek. 32:22, 24). Thus, some believe "Nephilim" means "fallen ones."

continual thought—that the giants were born as a result of sexual unions between the fallen angels and the women they took. However, diverging opinions arose about 1,000 years later due to a few church leaders becoming uncomfortable with the whole idea of fallen angels having sex with women.[29] Also, some modern scholars debate the ancient Jewish view on the origin of the giants and believe verse 4 mentions two separate events—that the Nephilim roamed the earth during the same time the "sons of God" took women and fathered children by them.

Before we disregard either of the two ancient views as too unusual, it's important to remember the Bible is full of supernatural events. For example:

1. Eve was deceived by a talking snake (Gen. 3:1–6).

2. Noah saved the animal kingdom by placing two of each species on a large boat (Gen. 7:7–11).

3. Moses spoke to God, who was in a bush that was on fire but didn't burn up (Exod. 3:2).

4. God parted a sea, and millions walked on dry ground to the other side (Exod. 12:37; 14:21–22).

29. See Chuck Missler, "Mischievous Angels or Sethites?," Koinonia House, August 1, 1997, https://www.khouse.org/articles/1997/110/. He succinctly explains, "It was in the 5th century A.D. that the 'angel' interpretation of Genesis 6 was increasingly viewed as an embarrassment when attacked by critics. (Furthermore, the worship of angels had begun within the church. Also, celibacy had also become an institution of the church. The 'angel' view of Genesis 6 was feared as impacting these views.) Celsus and Julian the Apostate used the traditional 'angel' belief to attack Christianity. Julius Africanus resorted to the Sethite interpretation as a more comfortable ground. Cyril of Alexandria also repudiated the orthodox 'angel' position with the 'line of Seth' interpretation. Augustine also embraced the Sethite theory and thus it prevailed into the Middle Ages. It is still widely taught today among many churches who find the literal 'angel' view a bit disturbing. There are many outstanding Bible teachers who still defend this view."

5. The Israelites ate bread that fell from the sky (Exod. 16:4).

6. They also drank water that spewed from a rock (Exod. 17:6).

7. A donkey talked to a man (Num. 22:27–31).

8. Joshua made time stand still (Josh. 10:12–14).

9. Jesus turned water into wine (John 2:3–9).

10. Jesus walked on water (John 6:19).

11. He also fed thousands of people from someone's lunch (Matt. 15:33–38; John 6:9–13).

12. Several people came back from the dead upon Jesus's death (Matt. 27:51–52)—this last one sounds like a zombie apocalypse!

Examples like these validate why the ancient Jews and earliest Christians weren't alarmed that angels developed and acted on evil desires that further corrupted humanity. For the Bible itself is supernatural (2 Tim. 3:16; 2 Pet. 1:20–21).

MORE REBELLION—FAME-SEEKING HUMANS

So far we have reviewed two angelic rebellions in addition to the Fall of Adam and Eve—but there's one more to examine before we close. We read earlier humans became so evil that God destroyed them by a worldwide flood and then repopulated the earth through Noah and his family (Gen. 6:7–13, 18). He gave civilization another chance. Yet we are informed:

Now the whole world had one language and a common speech. . . . Then they said, "Come, let us build ourselves a city, with a tower that reaches to the heavens, so that we may make a name for ourselves. . . ." But the LORD came down to see the city and the tower the people were building. The LORD said, "If as one people speaking the same language they have begun to do this, then nothing they plan to do will be impossible for them. Come, let us go down and confuse their language so they will not understand each other." So the LORD scattered them from there over all the earth, and they stopped building the city. That is why it was called Babel—because there the LORD confused the language of the whole world. From there the LORD scattered them over the face of the whole earth. (Gen. 11:1, 4–9 NIV)

Why was God concerned about humans striving to build a tower? Like with Satan, it goes back to intent. The similarities in their statements are subtle clues the Tempter is, again, at work:

Satan (Isa. 14:13–14)	People at "Babel" (Gen. 11:4 NIV)
"I will ascend to heaven."	"Let us build . . . a tower that reaches to the heavens . . ."
"I will make myself like the Most High."	"so that we may make a name for ourselves."

HUMANITY'S PLIGHT BUT GOD'S RESCUE

God restarted humanity to prevent people from falling into an unrecoverable state of evil, as did the prior civilization necessitating the flood.[30] For humanity's long-term well-being,

---

30. It is very sobering to realize this fact. As a reminder, God destroyed the first humans by a flood because "the LORD observed the extent of human wickedness on the earth, and he saw that everything they thought or imagined was

God initiated three actions. First, He miraculously divided their single language into separate languages, causing them to disperse geographically. In Genesis 10, God had already divided the descendants of Noah into 70 nations, sometimes identified as the "Table of Nations."

Second, God delegated total oversight of the 70 nations to watchers within His divine council: "When the Most High assigned lands to the nations, when he divided up the human race, he established the boundaries of the peoples according to the number in his heavenly court" (Deut. 32:8 NLT).[31]

Third, God devised a plan to create a new nation to save all the others. As evidence, the Table of Nations ends with the introduction of Abram (Gen. 11:26–31). God promised him, "This is my covenant with you: You will be the father of many nations. No longer will you be called Abram [meaning "exalted father" in Hebrew]; your name will be Abraham, for I have made you a father of many nations" (17:4–5 NIV). From Abraham's lineage came the nation of

---

consistently and totally evil" (Gen. 6:5 NLT). Even the wisdom writers warn, "Whoever remains stiff-necked after many rebukes will suddenly be destroyed—without remedy" (Prov. 29:1 NIV). We see this theme repeated in the New Testament: "Since they thought it foolish to acknowledge God, he abandoned them to their foolish thinking and let them do things that should never be done. Their lives became full of every kind of wickedness" (Rom. 1:28–29 NLT). Also, it is grievous to read that in the "final days" people "still refused to repent of their evil deeds and turn to God. They continued to worship demons" (Rev. 9:20 NLT).

31. I used the NLT here because it is consistent with the Hebraic thought. The last phrase "in his heavenly court" is actually "sons of God [*elohim*]" in Hebrew and is translated "sons of God [*theos*]" in the Greek Septuagint. Yet some translations have "sons of Israel" versus "sons of God." However, there are three more reasons why this rendering is incorrect: (1) referring to Israel would be out of context because it did not exist at that time; (2) the historical book of Jasher referenced in Josh. 10:13 and 2 Sam. 1:18 supports "sons of God"; and (3) ancient literature confirms the "watcher" theology: the Greek philosopher Plato (c. 424–348 BC) declared, "Once upon a time the gods were taking over by lot the whole earth according to its regions" (Plato, *Critias* 109b).

Israel (Exod. 3:6), and from Israel came the Savior[32] of the world (Matt. 1:2–16).

During Jesus's earthly ministry, He symbolically sent out 70 disciples to demonstrate His desire to redeem the 70 nations (Luke 10:1, 17–19). After His death, resurrection, and ascension back to heaven, Jesus sent the promised gift of the Holy Spirit (Acts 1:4, 8–9). When His disciples were filled with the Holy Spirit, they miraculously spoke in the languages understood by citizens from "every nation under heaven" (2:4–11). This signified humanity's true union is to be found in Christ.

Therefore, all who submit to His Lordship prove themselves to be the children of Abraham (Gal. 3:7–14). The ancient prophecy declared of Jesus, "The scepter will not depart from Judah, nor the ruler's staff from between his feet, until he to whom it belongs shall come and the obedience of the nations shall be his" (Gen. 49:10 NIV; Rev. 12:5). This is why the citizens of heaven sing, "All nations will come and worship before you, for your righteous acts have been revealed" (Rev. 15:4 NIV).

In God's great love for us, He devised a wise plan. He destroyed the works of the devil by the atoning death of His beloved Son.[33] Amen.

---

32. The term *savior* is the equivalent of "Messiah" (Hebrew) and "Christ" (Greek).

33. 1 John 3:8.

5

THE CHIEF DEMON PLUS
TWO MORE ENEMIES

We determined in chapter 4 that the Bible doesn't tell us the exact origin of demons. The New Testament defines them as "the devil and his angels" (Matt. 25:41), and the Old Testament informs us of two angelic rebellions: (1) power-hungry Satan and (2) sex-craving angels. It also tells us how these sinister beings corrupted humans.

ENEMY #1—SATAN, AND HOW HE BECAME THE CHIEF DEMON

As we continue our journey, the next logical question is this: How did Satan become the chief demon? As a reminder, *satan* is strictly a term in the Old Testament for "adversary." By the time we reach the New Testament, the first fallen angel is identified as God's chief enemy. So he is given the proper

73

name "Satan."[1] The Bible never tells us why Satan was placed in charge of evil spirits. However, these scriptural references make it clear he is their leader:

1. Jesus refers to him as the ruler of demons (Matt. 12:24–26).[2]
2. Jesus refers to him as "the ruler of this world" (John 12:31; 14:30; 16:11).
3. Satan is declared to be the god of this age (2 Cor. 4:4; Eph. 2:2).
4. Jesus defines demons as the devil and his angels (Matt. 25:41; Rev. 12:7–9).
5. An angel[3] of Satan is sent to torment the Apostle Paul (2 Cor. 12:7–8).
6. The one "called the devil, or Satan, . . . leads the whole world astray" (Rev. 12:9 NIV).

Although the terms *ruler* and *god* (the lesser) are used to refer to Satan, he is still subject to the sovereignty of God.[4] As a reminder:

1. Satan is a created being (Ezek. 28:15);
2. Watchers were called "sons of God" because they served in God's royal court—the divine council;

1. As examples, here are some Hebrew to English references: "*the* serpent" [*ha nahash*] (Gen. 3:1); "*the* adversary" [*ha satan*] (Job 1:12; 2:1; Zech. 3:1–2). We do not refer to people as "the Steve" or "the Michelle."
2. In the Gospel of Matthew, the Pharisees express a belief in a chief demon when they use the phrase "prince of demons" (9:34). In 12:24–26, Jesus equates "Beelzebub" (also "Beelzebul") with Satan. In ancient languages, *ba'al* (lord) and *zeboul* (exalted dwelling) together mean "lord of heaven." For the latter, see Heiser, *Demons*, 177.
3. The Greek word *angelos* (angel) can also mean "messenger." Here, the immediate context indicates it is a supernatural being.
4. Matt. 28:18; Luke 22:31–32; John 19:10–11; Rev. 9:1.

3. The Greek word for "world"[5] used here refers to the dark realm of unbelievers—as Jesus declared, "If the world hates you, keep in mind that it hated me first" (John 15:18 NIV); and

4. The Greek word for "age"[6] refers to this fallen era of human existence: "[Jesus] gave himself for our sins to rescue us from the present evil age" (Gal. 1:4 NIV).

Satan's Character and Limitations

These other titles used in the New Testament for Satan tell us a lot about his nature:

1. Evil one (Matt. 13:19; John 17:15; Eph. 6:16);

2. Deceiver (2 John 1:7; Rev. 12:9);

3. Father of lies (John 8:44; 1 John 2:22);

4. Tempter (Matt. 4:3);

5. Murderer (John 8:44; 10:10);

6. Accuser (Rev. 12:10);[7] and

7. Slanderer (Greek: *diabolos* [devil]; Matt. 4:1–11; John 8:44).

These titles can be intimidating. However, Satan's abilities are limited. As noted above, he is *not* all-powerful—only God is (Job 42:1–2). He is *not* all-present (Matt. 4:11)[8]—

---

5. Greek: κόσμος (*kosmos*), "world" (Friberg, 16493).

6. Greek: αἰών (*aiōn*), "age, aeon" (Friberg, 788).

7. As an Old Testament parallel, Exod. 28:36–38 states that the high priest bore the guilt of the Israelites as he offered sacrifices for their atonement. Thus, in Zech. 3:1–2 we witness Satan standing ready to accuse the high priest.

8. This Scripture states Satan left Jesus, so he was no longer present there; thus, he is not present everywhere.

only God is (Jer. 23:24). He is also *not* all-knowing—neither he nor his demons realized Jesus's death would atone for the sins of the world:

> We declare God's wisdom, a mystery[9] [the gospel] that has been hidden and that God destined for our glory before time began. None of the rulers of this age [demons] understood it [the gospel], for if they had, they would not have crucified the Lord of glory. (1 Cor. 2:7–8 NIV)

Moreover, there is no example in the Bible of Satan reading someone's mind—only God does (Ps. 139:4). Furthermore:

Satan *can accuse* us but (Rev. 12:10),   he *cannot condemn* us (Rom. 8:1)!

Satan *can hinder* us but (1 Thess. 2:18),   he *cannot stop* us (Matt. 16:18)!

Satan *can lead us astray* but (Rev. 12:9),   he *cannot separate* us from God's love (Rom. 8:38–39)!

Last, it is worth repeating: Satan cannot own anyone's soul—he does not even own his own soul (Ezek. 18:4).

What Demons Do under Satan's Command

Since Satan is limited, he delegates responsibilities to other demons. How many are there? Even ancient literature declares, "If the eye was given permission to see, no creature would be able to withstand the abundance and [presence] of the demons and continue to live unaffected."[10] Think about

---

9. Greek: μυστήριον (*mystērion*), "mystery" (Friberg, 18793), is used by the Apostle Paul on most occasions to refer to the unfolding of the Gospel (Rom. 16:25; 1 Cor. 15:51; Eph. 3:3–4; Col. 1:25–27; 1 Tim. 3:16).

10. BT, Berakhot 6a.2.

all the felt evil in our world today and imagine this: 200 million more demons currently imprisoned in the abyss[11] will be released someday (Rev. 9:11–16).

The Bible informs us of several factors related to demons. Here are a few:

1. They differ in ranks (Rev. 9:11).
2. They vary in degrees of wickedness and aid each other (Matt. 12:44–45).
3. They exhibit supernatural strength and are more powerful than humans (Mark 5:4; 2 Pet. 2:11).
4. They are organized—governmental terms are used to describe their structuring and geographical responsibilities (Dan. 10:13, 20; Eph. 6:12; Col. 1:16).
5. They incite people to persecute believers (Rev. 2:10).
6. They serve as agents of punishment for disobedience (Judg. 9:22–24, 56–57; Rev. 9:16–20).
7. They can inflict people with illnesses and ailments (Matt. 9:33; Mark 5:2–5; Luke 13:11–16).

They also seek to inhabit people, but why? As shared in chapter 4, there was an ancient Jewish belief (among many) that demons are dead Nephilim. Some today who ascribe to that belief teach that these beings were born with human bodies, so they desired to live in other ones after their physical deaths. However, the Bible teaches that Satan himself

---

11. "Abyss" is another name for "underworld." Notice the angel descends from heaven to earth to access the underworld: "The fifth angel sounded his trumpet, and I saw a star that had fallen from the sky to the earth. The star was given the key to the shaft of the Abyss" (Rev. 9:1 NIV).

entered Judas (Luke 22:3) and later Ananias (Acts 5:3), so apparently fallen angels strive to inhabit people.[12]

Moreover, it appears God grants only *holy* angels the ability to materialize into a human body (Heb. 13:2). It is possible God removed this ability from the fallen angels after they violated protocol by defiling themselves with women (Gen. 6:4). Demons have spiritual but not physical bodies and tend to operate invisibly (Eph. 2:2),[13] yet they can physically reveal themselves (Matt. 4:1–11). They also display supernatural abilities to interact with the physical world and can even shape-shift: "Even Satan disguises himself as an angel of light" (2 Cor. 11:14).

Is it important to know the personal names of demons? Old Covenant theologians before Christ classified certain demons by names and traits.[14] However, this occurred less in the New Testament and rabbinic literature. As a result, modern demonologists are less interested in determining who demons are and more concerned with casting them out.[15]

12. It could be argued that Judas and later Ananias were inhabited not by Satan per se but by a demon under his command. However, this is not what the Scriptures literally say. Furthermore, the Bible gives an example of Satan delegating a duty to an evil spirit when the Apostle Paul specifies a messenger (or angel) of Satan tormented him (2 Cor. 12:7–8).

13. In the phrase "powers of the air," the Greek word *aēr* (air) refers to the air surrounding the earth or general air, per Johannes E. Louw and Eugene A. Nida, *Greek-English Lexicon of the New Testament: Based on Semantic Domains*, 2nd ed. (New York: United Bible Societies, 1989), entry 802. This form of the word is used only here. However, the general word is used six other times in the New Testament, where it refers to air in close proximity (breathable air; see Acts 22:23; 1 Cor. 9:26; 14:9). Thus, it can imply demons are real but invisible like air.

14. Gideon Bohak, "Jewish Exorcisms Before and After the Destruction of the Second Temple," in *Was 70 CE a Watershed in Jewish History? On Jews and Judaism Before and After the Destruction of the Second Temple*, ed. Daniel S. Schwartz and Zeev Weiss (Leiden, the Netherlands: Brill, 2012), 280. For example, the book of Tobit notes a demon named "Ashmedai" who is still referenced today. Other ancient Jewish texts include 1 Enoch, Jubilees, and Josephus.

15. Eric Sorensen, Gideon Bohak, and Joseph Laycock, "Demons, Demonology," in *The Encyclopedia of the Bible and Its Reception*, vol. 6 of *Dabbesheth—Dreams and Dream Interpretation* (Berlin: de Gruyter, 2012), 541, 548, 568.

Why Satan Hates Humans

Satan displays hatred of all humans—believers and unbelievers—because it's his way of retaliating against God. There
are two times the Bible speaks of Satan being expelled from
heaven. One occurred during the beginnings of the First Creation (when he deceived Adam and Eve)[16] and the other at the
start of the New Creation (when Jesus atoned for humanity's sins).[17] Both expulsions involved Satan's direct attack on
humans.

Regarding the First Creation, the book of Genesis informs
us God created all people in His image and likeness (Gen.
1:26–27). Though scholars debate the exact meaning of this,[18]
we can at least agree on the significance of the Hebrew terms
and what they imply. The Hebrew word for "image"[19] is used
also for statues (Num. 33:52; 2 Kings 11:18), and "likeness"[20]
is used also for replicas (2 Kings 16:10; 2 Chron. 4:3). In the
ancient world, a king erected a statue to display his dominion
over a region (Dan. 3:1–5). Likewise, Adam and Eve represented God's dominion over the earth when He positioned
them in the garden and gave them ruling duties.[21]

16. The Bible does not give us an exact time Satan was expelled from heaven
(Isa. 14:12), but his act of deceiving the first humans is coincidentally recorded
in the beginnings of the First Creation (Gen. 3:1–6).

17. The Bible declares, "Therefore, if anyone is in Christ, the new creation
has come: The old has gone, the new is here!" (2 Cor. 5:17 NIV). Christ Jesus
resurrected on Sunday, the first day of the week in keeping with the original first
day of creation beginning on Sunday (Gen. 1:5). Then God rested on Saturday
(the seventh day). See also Beale, *Book of Revelation*, 658.

18. Peter J. Gentry, "Kingdom through Covenant: Humanity as the Divine
Image," *Southern Baptist Journal of Theology* 12, no. 1 (Spring 2008): 23.

19. Hebrew: צֶלֶם (*selem*), "image" (Holladay, 7202).

20. Hebrew: דְּמוּת (*demuth*), "likeness" (Holladay, 1852).

21. Hans Walter Wolff, *Anthropology of the Old Testament* (Philadelphia:
Fortress, 1974), 160–61.

Therefore, the "image and likeness" of God convey His majesty.[22] Yet, through deception, Satan stole humanity's rule and became "the god of this world" (2 Cor. 4:4). However, through obedience, Jesus became a human and reclaimed that earthly majesty (Phil. 2:8–11). Initially, I'm sure it brought Satan and his demons great delight to instigate the betrayals and brutalities against Jesus, since He is the *true* "image of the invisible God" (Col. 1:15)—until they discovered their persecutions of Jesus led to their own demise, for "by his wounds we are healed" (Isa. 53:5 NIV).

So why does Jesus wait to fully establish His kingdom? He is patiently giving all humans a chance to accept His plan of salvation (Ezek. 18:23; 2 Pet. 3:9). He explains, "This gospel of the kingdom will be proclaimed throughout the whole world as a testimony to all nations, and then the end will come" (Matt. 24:14). It will also include a new earth, where the leaves of the Tree of Life will bring "healing to the nations" (Rev. 21:1; 22:2).

In regard to the New Creation, demons hate us because humans were granted an opportunity for atonement and demons were not. Imagine you're a fallen angel who sinned against God. He offers you no means for forgiveness and condemns you to everlasting punishment. Yet the people He created disobeyed Him too, and He went as far as to send His only begotten Son to atone for their sins through His sacrificial death. You would probably protest, right? That's exactly what Satan and his demons did. Look at these events leading up to it in Revelation 12:

22. Gentry, "Kingdom through Covenant," 32.

1. An Israelite woman (Mary)[23] is pregnant and about to give birth (vv. 1–2).

2. Satan stands by to kill her son after He's born (vv. 3–4).

3. She gives birth to God the Son, ruler of "all the nations" (v. 5).

4. God the Son ascends to heaven and sits on His throne (v. 5).

5. Satan makes war against Israel and the Christian remnant for three and a half years (vv. 6, 13–17).[24]

Again, Satan and his demons didn't realize Jesus's death would atone for humanity's sin and essentially end their rule (1 Cor. 2:8). Outraged, they stage a protest in heaven:[25]

Now war arose in heaven, Michael and his angels fighting against the dragon. And the dragon and his angels fought back, but he was defeated, and there was no longer any place for them in heaven. And the great dragon was thrown down, that ancient serpent, who is called the devil and Satan, the deceiver of the whole world—he was thrown down to the earth, and his angels were thrown down with him. And I heard a loud voice in heaven, saying, "Now the salvation and the power and the kingdom of our God and the authority of his Christ have come, for the accuser of our brothers has

23. Dr. Greg Beale interprets this woman as also representing the "faithful community" (*Book of Revelation*, 625).

24. Given the chronology of real historical events in this passage, this event could be a reference to the First Jewish War (AD 66–70), culminating in the destruction of the temple.

25. The next series of events is tied to prior events of Christ's birth, resurrection, and ascension. Thus, this passage is *not* describing the fall of Satan from Gen. 3. This is a protest/war in response to Jesus redeeming the nations.

been thrown down, who accuses them day and night before our God. And they have conquered him by the blood of the Lamb and by the word of their testimony. . . . But woe to you, O earth and sea, for the devil has come down to you in great wrath, because he knows that his time is short!" (Rev. 12:7–12)

The specific uses of Satan's titles "accuser" (v. 10) and "slanderer"[26] (v. 12) hint to why he led the angelic protest. From the Fall to the cross, he literally made a name for himself by presenting a record of people's sins and advocating for their rightful punishment. Satan's efforts are severely hampered now that God offers humans—and not demons—atonement.[27]

As a double defeat, Satan is cast out of heaven again and crashes to the ground, brushing off the dirt with a flaring temper—as we are warned. His rage is described by two Greek words: *mega* meaning "great" and *thumos* meaning "wrath"—mega wrath! This form of *thumos* is used only two other times in the New Testament, where it describes

1. intensified anger (Col. 3:8); and
2. Pharaoh's fury when Moses keeps demanding, "Let my people go" (Heb. 11:27–29).

The last verse of the passage in Revelation says, "The dragon became furious . . . and went off to make war . . . on those who keep the commandments of God and hold

26. Greek: διάβολος (*diabolos*), "devil" or "slanderer" (DANK, 1524).
27. Satan's accusatory function was not eliminated, for we read elsewhere, "Give the adversary no occasion for slander. For some have already strayed after Satan" (1 Tim. 5:14–15).

to the testimony of Jesus" (Rev. 12:17). On the heels of a failed protest and as he awaits his impending doom, Satan has declared "thermonuclear" war on Christians.

While God's mercy is magnificent, it's sobering to discover He extends it only to humans. Why? For one, Satan and his fellow demons played, and continue to play, a role in humanity's disobedience. And two, Jesus warns, "Someone who does not know, and then does something wrong, will be punished only lightly. When someone has been given much, much will be required in return; and when someone has been entrusted with much, even more will be required" (Luke 12:48 NLT). God expected more from those He entrusted to watch over His image bearers. Instead, each of their rebellions corrupted humanity. Therefore, God declares the fallen angels will suffer in hell's eternal flames (Matt. 25:41)—they will have no peace.

ENEMY #2–THE WORLD

Collectively, the Bible warns us of three main enemies: Satan, the world, and the flesh. Satan is a proven enemy, but how is the world a foe? When the Bible mentions the world, the context determines whether it is referencing (1) creation; (2) unbelievers; or (3) the realm of unbelievers. For example, it is written of Jesus, "He was in the world [realm], and the world [creation] was made through Him, and the world [unbelievers] did not know Him" (John 1:10 NASB).

What makes the world a danger to Christians? Well, the concern isn't creation, because God declared it to be good (Gen. 1:31). The threat is unbelievers and how their environment opposes God in various ways.[28] Let's look at eight biblical facts about unbelievers:

1. They are loved by God, who desires a right relationship with them (John 3:16; Col. 1:20–22).
2. They are created in God's image like all people (Gen. 1:26–27).
3. They are called "sons of disobedience" (Eph. 2:2; 5:6).
4. They are called "children of the devil" (1 John 3:10).
5. They are prone to crave sin over righteousness (John 3:19).
6. They can corrupt godly character (1 Cor. 15:33; 2 Cor. 6:14–18).
7. They can incite hatred toward Jesus and His followers (John 15:18–20; James 4:4).
8. They are in collusion with Satan (1 John 5:18–19).[29]

Before you sell your possessions and move into isolation, recall this: "Among these we all once lived in the passions of our flesh . . . so we were by nature children of wrath, like

28. Interestingly, here are five parallels between the unbelieving world and the ungodly. They (1) were atoned for by Jesus's death (Rom. 4:5; 5:6); (2) make up society (1 Cor. 6:1); (3) are opposite the children of God (1 Pet. 4:18; 2 Pet. 2:5); (4) can corrupt character (2 Tim. 2:16; Jude 4); and (5) will be punished (2 Pet. 2:6; 3:7; Jude 15).

29. Verses 18–19 distinguish believers from unbelievers. In verse 18, the form of the Greek verb *hapto* (touch) is used elsewhere only in Luke 7:39 referring to the repentant woman who gratefully washes Jesus's feet with her hair and tears. Thus, it is the idea of a relationship. The Bible declares Satan cannot have a relationship with a true believer. Also, verse 19 literally reads, "The whole world in the evil one lies/reclines [*keimai*]." The words *touch* and *recline* used in proximity to unbelievers is a strong indication of alliance—also intimacy (even unknowingly).

the rest of mankind" (Eph. 2:3 RSV). Also, since God loves unbelievers, He calls us not to abandon those in darkness but to be a light to them (Matt. 5:14).

Another danger with the world is it attracts us to what God forbids: "For all that is in the world—the lust of the flesh, the lust of the eyes, and the pride of life—is not from the Father but is from the world" (1 John 2:16, author's translation from Greek).[30] Satan is the agent of temptation, and the world remains the object. The avenues are our three main desires: what looks good, feels good, and brings good. When Satan tempted Eve with the forbidden fruit, she reasoned that it was appealing, appetizing, and advantageous.

Three Avenues of Temptation

The First Temptation (Gen. 3:6)	Now All Temptations (1 John 2:16)	
1. Eve saw that the tree was beautiful.	1. Lust of the eyes	(Looks good!)
2. Its fruit looked delicious.	2. Lust of the flesh	(Feels good!)
3. She wanted the wisdom it would grant.	3. Pride of life	(Brings good!)

Temptation competes against what God already said is good!
(Gen. 1:4, 10, 12, 18, 21, 25, 31)

Every temptation is based on a lie. When we yield to a forbidden desire, disaster befalls us—as it did Eve, then Adam. Since temptation is limited to three main avenues, the Tempter's scheme remains the same—for everyone. In Matthew 4, we learn he even had the audacity to use it on Jesus!

---

30. Stephen S. Smalley, *1, 2, 3 John* (Waco: Word, 1984), 81. Dr. Smalley confirms the use of *kosmos* (world) refers to "human society, temporarily controlled by the power of evil, organized in opposition to God. . . . [This] is the meaning which 'kosmos' carries in this verse [15] and vv 16–17 (where the word occurs six times in all)."

Matthew 4:1–11 Compared to Deuteronomy 6:13, 16; and 8:2, 16

Temptations	Satan's Attempts	Jesus's Responses
Lust of the flesh	"Turn this stone into bread."	"Obeying God ultimately satisfies."
Pride of life	"Demonstrate your abilities."	"No need to test the limits of God's Word."
Lust of the eyes	"I'll relinquish the world, if you worship me."	"Nothing takes the place of God."

Jesus conquered each temptation with a dagger stab from Scripture. He is our example. This is why the Bible encourages us, "For we do not have a High Priest who cannot sympathize with our weaknesses, but was in all points tempted as we are, yet without sin" (Heb. 4:15 NKJV). More promising, the Bible assures us that the avenues of temptation are "common to mankind. And God is faithful; he will not let you be tempted beyond what you can bear. . . . He will also provide a way out so that you can endure it" (1 Cor. 10:13 NIV). As it is proclaimed, "Who is it that overcomes the world? Only the one who believes that Jesus is the Son of God" (1 John 5:5 NIV).

ENEMY #3—THE FLESH

Last, we discuss our third and final enemy—the flesh. Modern Bible versions translate it as "sinful nature" because it refers to the physical body's corruption by sin at the Fall. This condition is so serious the Bible warns us, "Abstain from fleshly desires that war against the soul" (1 Pet. 2:11, author's translation from Greek). Listen to how sin infected the mind (thoughts) and heart (emotions):

1. The heart is deceitful, incurable, and cannot be understood without God (Jer. 17:9).
2. The heart can lead to destructive ends (Prov. 14:12).
3. The heart must be guarded as a top priority to avoid it poisoning one's life (Prov. 4:23).[31]
4. The mind is hostile to God and refuses to submit to His will (Rom. 8:7; Col. 1:21).
5. The mind must accept truth to be cured (Matt. 4:17; John 8:32). Note: the Greek word translated "repent" is a combination of two Greek words—*meta* (change) and *noeō* (thinking).
6. The mind must enforce obedience to Christ (2 Cor. 10:3–5).
7. The mind requires scriptural renewal for behavioral change (Rom. 12:2).

Overall, the flesh is hazardous. "For the desires of the flesh are against the Spirit, and the desires of the Spirit are against the flesh, for these are opposed to each other, to keep you from doing the things you want to do" (Gal. 5:17). Without Christ, we are born physically alive but spiritually dead. This is why we must be spiritually reborn; it enables us to fulfill the prior verse: "Walk by the Spirit, and you will not gratify the desires of the flesh" (5:16).

When I embarked on writing this book, I initially focused on demons as the source of evil in our world. Then I was slapped back into reality by this verse: "People ruin their lives by their own foolishness and then are angry at the LORD"

---

31. A wellspring is a metaphor for the heart. As a source of water, it can refresh our lives. However, if it becomes corrupted, it can poison us too.

(Prov. 19:3 NLT). I'm also disturbed every time I read, "God made humanity virtuous, but they, themselves, pursued many schemes" (Eccles. 7:29, author's translation from Hebrew). The reflexive use of "they" emphasizes our willful decision to forsake our good nature to pursue evil plans. Also, the root word in Hebrew for "schemes" is found in Genesis 6:5, where it's translated "thoughts":[32] "The LORD saw that the wickedness of man was great in the earth, and that every intention of the *thoughts* of his heart was only evil continually." Surely, we impress demons with some of the evils we ourselves invent.

Let us not be deceived! We are without excuse if we do not use our inkling of freedom to seek God. The Bible guarantees, "The LORD searches every heart and understands every desire and every thought. If you seek him, he will be found by you" (1 Chron. 28:9 NIV). The Apostle Paul diagnoses the problem and then poses the solution: "Wretched man that I am! Who will deliver me from this body of death? Thanks be to God through Jesus Christ our Lord!" (Rom. 7:24–25).

---

32. Tremper Longman III, *Book of Ecclesiastes* (Grand Rapids: Eerdmans, 1998), 207.

6

15 POINTS OF CLARITY ABOUT EXPELLING DEMONS

D ue to differing views on the topic of confronting demons, here are 15 points of clarity.

1. THE WORD *EXORCISM* IS NOT USED IN THE BIBLE.

The actual Greek word means "cast out or expel."[1] The word *exorcise* can technically mean this. However, people associate exorcisms with horror movies that overdramatize them and foster an ungodly fear of demons (2 Tim. 1:7). So many Christian leaders opt to use the phrase "deliverance ministry" or "freedom session" when liberating a person from evil spirits.

2. THE TERM *DEMON POSSESSION* IS NOT FOUND IN THE BIBLE.

The phrase *demon possession* was first coined by Flavius Josephus (a first-century Jewish historian), then it was later

1. Greek: ἐκβάλλω (*ekballō*), "to cast out" or "to expel" (Friberg, 8353).

integrated into church language.[2] However, it is an inaccurate translation because it wrongly conveys ownership. For example, if a thief breaks into your home, it doesn't mean he now owns your property. Likewise, Satan doesn't own anyone (Ezek. 18:4). This is another reason Jesus refers to him as a thief (John 10:10).

The precise word is *demonized*, meaning to "experience inward control by a hostile spirit."[3] Some well-meaning Christians use "demonically influenced" because that idea is more acceptable. However, it, too, falls short of the actual meaning. As Dr. Jeffrey J. Niehaus, a professor of Old Testament at Gordon-Conwell Theological Seminary, explains, "I can be attacked, influenced, or deceived by another human, but that does not mean that human is inside me."[4] Separate from the word *demonized*, the Greek uses different words to describe being tempted, hindered, oppressed, or embattled in spiritual warfare.

The specific Greek word for *demonized* is used 13 times in 10 different cases[5] and always refers to someone inhabited by a demon. Also, the Bible uses other Greek phrases to identify demonized victims. Since the English translations vary, here are the renderings:

1. Having an unclean spirit (Mark 1:23; 5:2; 7:25; Luke 4:33; Acts 8:7);

2. Having the spirit of an unclean demon (Luke 4:33);

2. Alfred Edersheim, *The Life and Times of Jesus the Messiah*, vol. 1 (Peabody, MA: Hendrickson, 1995), 479.

3. Greek: δαιμονίζομαι (*daimonizomai*), demonized (DANK, 1408).

4. Jeffrey J. Niehaus, email discussion with author, June 16, 2023.

5. Matt. 4:24; 8:16, 28–33; 9:32; 12:22; 15:22; Mark 1:32; 5:15–18; Luke 8:36; John 10:21.

3. Having a mute spirit (Mark 9:17);

4. Having demons (Luke 8:27);

5. Having a spirit of divination (Acts 16:16);

6. Having an evil spirit (Acts 19:13); and

7. Being afflicted by an unclean spirit (Acts 5:16).[6]

Demonization can range from a mild case, like the woman of faith with the crippling back ailment caused by a demon (Luke 13:11, 16), to a severe one similar to the man isolated from society due to his uncontrollable behavior (8:27–29).

3. THE BIBLE DISTINGUISHES REGULAR ILLNESSES FROM ONES CAUSED BY DEMONS.

Jesus expelled an epileptic-causing demon from a man (Matt. 17:15–18). However, in another place, epilepsy and other health issues are distinguished from those who are demonized (4:24). In this book, multiple examples will be given of people whose physical and mental health issues were the result of being demonized—many of whom were unaware demons were the source of their problems.

4. CHRISTIANS DO NOT NEED A SPECIAL SPIRITUAL GIFT TO EXPEL DEMONS.

Some believe expelling demons falls under the category of healing, since:

6. Separate from the list of victims, opponents of Jesus accuse Him six times of having a demon (Mark 3:30; John 7:20; 8:48, 49, 52; 10:20). Also, they allege this twice of John the Baptist (Matt. 11:18; Luke 7:33).

1. Both actions are sometimes listed in the same verse (Matt. 4:24);

2. Having a demon expelled results in better mental and/or physical health (Luke 6:18; 8:2);

3. Healing is listed as a spiritual gift not given to all Christians (1 Cor. 12:9, 28, 30);

4. The ability to distinguish between good and evil spirits is a spiritual gift (1 Cor. 12:10); and

5. In the third and fourth centuries, the independent ministry of expelling demons was deferred to trusted believers who were identified to have the gift of healing;[7] in 1972, the Roman Catholic Church made it a responsibility for only their priests.[8]

However, the gift of healing is typically distinguished from the ability to expel demons:

1. "Behold, I cast out demons and perform cures" (Luke 13:32).

2. "And [Jesus] called the 12 together and gave them power and authority over all demons and to cure diseases" (Luke 9:1).

3. "And he healed many who were sick with various diseases, and cast out many demons" (Mark 1:34).

7. *Apostolic Tradition* 20.3, from Burton Scott Easton, trans., *The Apostolic Tradition of Hippolytus* (Cambridge: Cambridge University Press, 1934). Also, he states in footnote 15, "Healers in the specialized form of 'exorcists' form a minor order in Rome a generation later [fourth century]. One of their most important functions was to assist in preparing catechumens [new converts] for baptism."

8. "Appointment of Exorcists in the Catholic Church," The Rosary Foundation, accessed January 17, 2024, https://exorcismus.org/appointment-of-exorcists-in-the-catholic-church.

When Jesus and His disciples expelled demons, they used only verbal commands. However, the biblical examples we see of healing typically involve two actions: laying on of hands and anointing with oil.

1. "[Jesus] laid his hands on a few sick people and healed them" (Mark 6:5).
2. "And they cast out many demons and anointed with oil many who were sick and healed them" (Mark 6:13).
3. "All those who had any who were sick with various diseases brought them to [Jesus], and he laid his hands on every one of them and healed them" (Luke 4:40).
4. "Is anyone among you sick? Let him call for the elders of the church, and let them pray over him, anointing him with oil in the name of the Lord" (James 5:14).

While the gift of distinguishing between spirits can aid those assisting a demonized person, it, too, is unique and distinct from the ability to expel demons. As Bible scholar Dr. Wayne Grudem attests:

As with all spiritual gifts, it would seem that there are degrees of intensity or strength in the development of this gift [of distinguishing between spirits] as well. So some may have this gift developed to a very high degree and others may find it functioning only occasionally. Moreover, in the lives of all believers, there may be something analogous to this gift, some kind of ability to sense in their spirits the presence of the Holy Spirit or to sense demonic influence from time to time in other people.[9]

To eradicate false teachers, around the third century church leaders brought the practice of expelling demons under the direct oversight of the church and assigned it as a duty for those with the demonstrated gift of healing.[10] For instance:

1. There was no ordination for a person with the gift of healing because it was considered an ability a typical Christian could have.[11]

2. There was no church office for an "exorcist" until the fourth century, yet expelling demons was still being practiced beforehand (see point 5).[12]

3. Baptism under Jesus and the Apostles was usually conducted immediately after a person professed faith. However, early church leaders later began to postpone baptism to upward of three years to ensure a new convert wasn't demonized and fully

9. Wayne Grudem, *Systematic Theology* (Grand Rapids: Zondervan, 1994), 426.

10. While it's natural for us to want to protect the sanctity of the church, Jesus had a concern with this approach (Mark 9:39; Luke 9:50).

11. *Apostolic Tradition* 15.1.

12. Arthur Cushman McGiffert, trans., *Historia Ecclesiae (Church History of Eusebius)* (Cincinnati: Lane Theological Seminary, 1890), 736n2125: "The Exorcists likewise constituted one of the inferior orders of the clergy; but although we find exorcism very frequently referred to by the Fathers of the second century, there seems to have been no such office until the third century, the present being the earliest distinct reference to it. In the fourth century we find the office in all parts of the Church East and West. Their duty was to take charge of those supposed to be possessed of an evil spirit; to pray with them, care for them, and exorcise the demon when possible."

understood the Gospel. This was an effort to alleviate false teaching by confirming a person's faith before the church endorsed them as a Christian.[13]

Thus, the Bible and the early church distinguish the ability
to expel demons from the gift of healing.

5. JESUS GRANTS ALL CHRISTIANS THE ABILITY TO EXPEL DEMONS.

The authority to expel demons was first given to the 12 disciples (Luke 9:1), then expanded to the 72 disciples (10:1,
17). These three reasons confirm why all of Jesus's followers
have this default ability in Christ:

1. The Gospels record a man expelling demons who
   was unknown to either the 12 or the 72 disciples.
   One of them tried to stop him, but Jesus corrected
   him: "'Teacher, we saw someone using your name to
   cast out demons, but we told him to stop because he
   wasn't in our group.' 'Don't stop him!' Jesus said"
   (Mark 9:38–39 NLT).
2. Philip was in neither group, but he, too, expelled demons (Acts 8:6–8).
3. It is important to note that early Christian leaders
   understood it as a general ability among Christians:
   a. Justin Martyr (c. AD 100–165): "[Jesus] said, 'I
      give unto you power to tread on serpents, and on

---

13. *Apostolic Tradition* 16.8, 9–24; 17.1. Proof of a change in protocols can be
seen by reviewing Matt. 28:18–20, where Jesus instructs the Apostles to baptize
(first), then teach new converts the Scriptures (afterward). Hippolytus instructed the
inverse in an effort to authenticate Christian character before church endorsement.

scorpions . . . and on all the might of the enemy.'
And now we, who believe on our Lord Jesus, who
was crucified under Pontius Pilate, when *we exorcise all demons and evil spirits, have them sub-
jected to us.*"[14]

b. Origen (c. AD 185–253): "It is not by incantations that *Christians seem to prevail [over evil
spirits], but by the name of Jesus*, accompanied
by the announcement of the narratives [Gospels]
which relate to him; for the repetition of these has
frequently been the means of *driving demons out
of men*, especially when those who repeated them
did so in a sound and genuinely believing spirit."[15]

c. Athanasius (c. AD 293–373), regarding expelling demons as proof of the resurrection: "And how does it
happen, if [Christ] is not risen. . . . For where Christ
is mentioned, and faith in him, all idolatry is eradi-
cated, all demonic deceit is revealed, and *no demon
even tolerates that the name is mentioned, but hur-
ries to flee, as it hears it mentioned.*"[16]

Thus, expelling demons isn't limited to any one group of
Jesus's followers.

6. NO SPECIAL FORMULA IS NEEDED TO EXPEL DEMONS.

Jesus only commanded demons to leave:

14. Justin Martyr, *Dialogue* 76:6, emphasis added.
15. Origen, *Contra Celsum* 1:6, emphasis added.
16. Athanasius, *On the Incarnation (Der Incarnatione Verbi)*, 32, emphasis
added.

- "Jesus rebuked him, saying, 'Be silent, and come out of him!'" (Mark 1:25).
- "[Jesus] rebuked the impure spirit. '. . . I command you, come out of him'" (Mark 9:25 NIV).

Early church leader Origen (c. AD 185–253) observed,

> [Christians expel demons] without the use of any curious magic, or incantations, but merely by prayer and simple adjurations which *the plainest person can use*. Because for the most part it is *unlettered persons who perform this work*: thus making manifest the grace which is in the word of Christ, and the despicable weakness of demons, which, in order to be overcome and driven out of the bodies and souls of men, *do not require the power and wisdom of those who are mighty in argument, and most learned in matters of faith*.[17]

Again, no special formula or advanced training is necessary for a Christian to expel demons. Yet it's always wise to seek advice from those with experience (Prov. 15:22).

7. THE EFFECTIVENESS OF EXPELLING DEMONS CAN BE HINDERED BY A LACK OF SPIRITUAL CONDITIONING.

Our spiritual condition can affect our ability to expel demons. The disciples experienced regular success because they were spiritually fit. However, one day a father approached Jesus because the disciples failed to expel a demon from his son: "Jesus said, 'You faithless and corrupt people!' . . . Then Jesus rebuked the demon in the boy, and it left him. . . .

17. Origen, *Contra Celsum* 7:4, emphasis added.

Afterward the disciples asked Jesus privately, 'Why couldn't we cast out that demon?' 'You don't have enough faith,' Jesus told them" (Matt. 17:17–20 NLT). In Mark's edition of the Gospel, Jesus adds, "This kind cannot be driven out by anything but prayer" (Mark 9:29).

In the Greek, this reads as a phrase: "in prayer."[18] This exact phrase is used only here in the New Testament. Nevertheless, it is used six other times in the Greek Septuagint, where it refers to personal petitions versus intercessory prayer.[19] Later copyists included the phrase "and fasting"[20] to the above verse because ancient believers often fasted during periods of earnest prayer. This indicates early Christians understood Jesus to emphasize (1) demons have differing strengths; and (2) believers need to observe regular times for personal prayer to be in the proper spiritual condition to resolve the more severe cases of demonization.

So staying spiritually fit is a top priority:

1. The Bible instructs, "All the believers devoted themselves to the apostles' teaching, and to fellowship, and to sharing in meals (including the Lord's Supper), and to [the] prayer" (Acts 2:42 NLT).
2. The Apostle Paul adds, "Physical training is good, but training for godliness is much better, promising benefits in this life and in the life to come" (1 Tim. 4:8 NLT).

18. The Greek phrase is ἐν προσευχῇ (*en proseuchē*).
19. Referred to for linguistic reasons only. See 1 Macc. 5:33; Sir. 7:14; 39:5–6; 50:19; 51:13. This literature is known as the Deuterocanonicals—books written during the period between the Old Testament and the New Testament.
20. The King James Version relied on this later Greek manuscript, but the phrase is not found in the most reliable ones.

3. Jesus even warns, "Don't rejoice because evil spirits obey you; rejoice because your names are registered in heaven" (Luke 10:20 NLT).

Also, there is a historical account confirming the biblical importance of spiritual conditioning. There were some ancient rabbis who tried to expel a demon from a haunted building, but they had no success. A very pious rabbi was traveling through the area, so they tricked him into staying in the building. The demon appeared to him in the middle of the night. However, unlike the other rabbis, this pious rabbi successfully expelled it. This experience validated, even among Old Covenant believers, the importance of one's spiritual fitness when confronting evil spirits.[21]

8. JESUS SUCCESSFULLY CONTENDED WITH DEMONS SO THAT WE CAN VICTORIOUSLY DO THE SAME—IN HIS NAME.

Until Jesus returns (Rev. 19:11–16), we remain in a spiritual war (Eph. 6:12). Nevertheless, we are victors because Jesus won the victory (Col. 2:15). This is why He also promises us that demons cannot harm us when we are expelling them (Luke 10:19).

9. IT IS BIBLICAL TO REBUKE A DEMON—AS JESUS DID.

Some leaders claim Jude 9 teaches we shouldn't rebuke demons: "When the archangel Michael, contending with the devil, was disputing about the body of Moses, he did not

21. BT, Kiddushin 29b.13.

presume to pronounce a blasphemous judgment, but said, 'The Lord rebuke you.'"

However, expelling demons is not even a point of discussion in this verse. Also, verses 8 and 10 indicate the actual concern is about the bad character of false teachers. Also, Jude appears to be using the Archangel Michael as an example of how to honor church authority. For instance, it was God's prerogative of what to do with Moses's body, so Michael deferred to the Lord on that matter.

Now, on the topic of expelling demons, Jesus rebuked demons when He expelled them (Mark 1:25; 9:25). Thus, His disciples would have naturally done the same when He authorized them to expel demons (Luke 9:1; 10:1, 17). So not rebuking demons would contradict the ministry Jesus Himself ordained. Additionally, examples in the previous points from the Bible and early church history verify Jesus and His followers rebuked demons. Therefore, believers are well within their Christ-given authority to do so.

A second argument teaches that James 4:7 doesn't require us to rebuke demons but only to "submit yourselves therefore to God. Resist the devil, and he will flee from you." However, it overlooks two facts: (1) James bases his words on Jesus's temptation (Matt. 4:1–11); and (2) Jesus demonstrates that resisting the devil may involve commanding him to depart.

Temptation	Jesus's Response
1. "If you are the Son of God, command these stones to become bread."	"It is written . . ."
2. "If you are the Son of God, throw yourself down [from the top of the temple] . . ."	"It is written . . ."
3. "If you will fall down and worship me, I will give you the world."	"'Be gone, Satan! For it is written . . .' Then the devil left him."

In all three temptations, Jesus "submitted to God" and "resisted the devil." Yet He still *commanded* Satan to leave. Remember, whenever we encounter demons, we're in an active battle. Thus, James 4:7 doesn't prohibit us from rebuking demons or alleviate the need to do so—especially when they are persistent.

10. IT IS BIBLICAL TO BIND DEMONS—AS JESUS EXEMPLIFIES.

It's argued that the terms *bind* (prohibit) and *loose* (permit) refer to strictly legal matters.[22] Jesus uses them that way when He grants the 12 disciples authority on matters of Christian accountability. He tells them that if offenders "still refuse to listen, tell it to the church; and if they refuse to listen even to the church, treat them as you would a pagan or a tax collector. Truly I tell you, whatever you bind on earth will be bound in heaven, and whatever you loose on earth will be loosed in heaven" (Matt. 18:17–18 NIV).

However, these terms—especially *bind*—aren't limited to just legal matters. The same Greek word is used when referring to the demonized man whom no one could physically bind (Mark 5:3). Additionally, Jesus uses the word *bind* in the context of expelling demons:

> If it is by the Spirit of God that I cast out demons, then the kingdom of God has come upon you. Or how can someone enter a strong man's house and plunder his goods, unless he first *binds* the strong man? Then indeed he may plunder his house. (Matt. 12:28–29)

22. Josephus, *Jewish Wars* 1:110. Under Queen Alexandra of Jerusalem, the Pharisees "became the administrators of all public affairs, empowered to banish and readmit whom they pleased, as well as to loose and to bind."

Binding was also used in ancient Jewish exorcisms as documented in archaeological discoveries.[23] So there is no biblical reason it cannot be used if the Christian discerns it to be necessary.

As an example, I had a wonderful supervisor who went on an extended vacation, and he left me in charge of the office in his absence. Since I have expertise in organizational management, I enhanced a few processes and implemented some time-saving efficiencies. When he returned, he found an empty inbox, lighter workloads, and a cheerful staff. Initially, he was very pleased with the improvements. However, his joy mysteriously turned into suspicion as he began to question my motives. This was unlike him. Sensing this was a spiritual warfare tactic, I uttered a binding prayer: "Father, you commanded us to pray for those in authority over us that we may live peaceful and quiet lives [1 Tim. 2:1–2]. I ask You as the highest authority to bind and cast away every evil spirit that is striving to deceive my supervisor by sowing seeds of distrust in me. From this day forward, grant him Your spiritual discernment to distinguish their voices and implanted thoughts from his own in order to expose their lies and secure my peace with him. In Jesus's Name, amen."[24]

---

23. Gideon Bohak, "Expelling Demons and Attracting Demons in Jewish Magical Texts," in *Experiencing the Beyond: Intercultural Approaches*, ed. Gert Melville and Carlos Ruta (Berlin: de Gruyter, 2018), 172: "Just as the [incantation] bowls' texts seek to expel, or bind, a whole host of demons, the bowls' iconography too seeks to bind them in strong chains, and prevent them from harming their potential victims."

24. The use of "I bind" or "God bind" is jurisdictional. Those experienced in the ministry of expelling demons attest they tend to have more success when they follow scriptural lines of authority. The phrase "I bind" works in these four cases: (1) spouse to spouse (1 Cor. 7:3–4); (2) parent to child under their care (Matt. 17:15–18; 1 Cor. 7:14); (3) church leader to church member (Heb. 13:17); and (4) one willing believer to another (Gal. 6:2). Since my supervisor was in

The next day, my supervisor (who's skeptical of anything supernatural) scheduled a private meeting with me. After gathering his thoughts, he shared, "I don't want you to think I'm out of my mind, but I had a very weird experience yesterday. I saw an email from you to the staff where you updated them on the project I have you overseeing. You followed the right protocols, but I couldn't understand why I was so bothered by it. Then I heard a voice over my shoulder insinuate, 'He's trying to sabotage you.' I immediately rebuked it and told it to go away, because you've been extremely loyal to me."

Subsequently, he entrusted me with even more leadership responsibilities, submitted me for a promotion, and took a longer vacation! To date, he's still one of the best bosses I ever had.

11. EXPELLING DEMONS IS NOT ALWAYS INSTANTANEOUS.

The Greek verb structure and chronology of events in Mark 5:5–13 indicate some demons were not expelled instantly—even by Jesus:

1. The demonized man of the Gadarene region saw Jesus from afar and was terrified, "For [Jesus] had said[25] to him, 'Come out of the man, you unclean spirit!'" (v. 8 RSV).

---

authority over me (Rom. 13:1), I appealed to God as the highest authority. When in doubt, use "God bind."

25. The Greek tense and mood of *lego* (to say) is in the imperfect indicative. Per Greek scholar Dr. William D. Mounce, "[It] expresses linear action in past time. That action may be repetitive, prolonged or just beginning. Sometimes,

2. However, the demon did not leave.

3. Next, Jesus asked for his name, and it replied, "My name is Legion, for we are many" (v. 9).

4. Then they begged Jesus to send them into the swine (vv. 10–12).

5. After Jesus authorized them, they departed into the swine (v. 13).

Experienced church leaders Grayson Ensign and Edward Howe confirm expelling demons can be a process—especially in a counseling setting where one strives to unravel the historical circumstances that brought about the client's condition. "The Lord has graciously led us into more effective prayers against evil spirits which resulted in a dramatic cut in the time needed for deliverance. . . . Now sessions last approximately two hours and accomplish much more than we were able to do in the previous four or five hours."[26]

12. JESUS EXPELLING DEMONS BY "A WORD" MEANS HE DID SO "VERBALLY."

The Gospels record Jesus casting out demons "with a word" (Matt. 8:16). Obviously, Jesus used more than one word, because he used eight (five in Greek) when he commanded the legion of demons, "Come out of the man, you unclean

---

however, the imperfect expresses repeated *attempts*" (Mounce, *Basics of Biblical Greek* [Grand Rapids: Zondervan, 1993], 176).

26. Grayson H. Ensign and Edward Howe, *Bothered? Bewildered? Bewitched? Your Guide to Practical Supernatural Healing* (Cincinnati: Recovery Publications, 1984), 180.

spirit!" (Mark 5:8). The Greek phrase is used two other times in the Gospel of Matthew, when

1. the centurion asks Jesus to command his servant from afar to be healed (8:8); and
2. the Pharisees try to trap Jesus in what He says (22:15).

Therefore, the phrase emphasizes Jesus's power to expel demons merely by command. In contrast, this was drastically different from the practice of other religious leaders in His day. Historical evidence shows ancient Jews relied on three main methods to expel demons: (1) natural substances—including minerals, roots, and organs from certain fish; (2) prayers, incantations, along with commands; and (3) help from other leaders with godly reputations or who were deemed to have experience.[27]

13. UNREPENTANCE ALLOWS A DEMON TO ENTER AND RE-ENTER—IN GREATER FORCE.

In Matthew 12:41–45, Jesus warns of the danger of unrepentance. Under the Old Covenant, God warned Israel it would come under the rule of foreign invaders due to unrepentance (Deut. 28:48–49). Later, the Prophet Jeremiah announced the coming of a New Covenant due to Israel breaking the old one (Jer. 31:31–33). Now, in the context of the Romans occupying the nation, Jesus ushers in the New Covenant

27. Gideon Bohak, "Jewish Exorcisms Before and After the Destruction of the Second Temple," 281–84.

(Luke 22:20), but the religious leaders keep rejecting Him. This is why He warns:

> The men of Nineveh will rise up at the judgment with this generation and condemn it, for they repented at the preaching of Jonah, and behold, something greater than Jonah is here. The queen of the South will rise up at the judgment with this generation and condemn it, for she came from the ends of the earth to hear the wisdom of Solomon, and behold, something greater than Solomon is here.
>
> When the unclean spirit has gone out of a person, it passes through waterless places seeking rest, but finds none. Then it says, "I will return to my house from which I came." And when it comes, it finds the house empty, swept, and put in order. Then it goes and brings with it seven other spirits more evil than itself, and they enter and dwell there, and the last state of that person is worse than the first. So also will it be with this evil generation. (Matt. 12:41–45; see also Luke 11:23–26)

Many Christians misinterpret Matthew 12:44. They incorrectly conclude that the expelled demon returning to find the house "empty, swept, and put in order" means the person failed to move God into the house, resulting in the person being redemonized. However, Jesus couldn't have had this idea in mind, because the promise of the Holy Spirit's indwelling didn't occur until after His death, resurrection, and ascension.[28] Moreover, by expelling unclean spirits, Jesus and

28. The promised Holy Spirit came on the first Pentecost after the death, resurrection, and ascension of Christ. For the Jews, the day of Pentecost is the anniversary of God giving Moses the Ten Commandments on Mount Sinai—the Old Covenant. Regarding the New Covenant, the Prophet Jeremiah declares, "Behold, the days are coming, declares the LORD, when I will make a New Covenant ·

His disciples were literally "cleaning up" Israelite society. Thus, the expelled demon simply observes the effectiveness of that ministry as evidenced by the "house" still cleansed of evil spirits.

Therefore, Jesus's concern is their unrepentance. Unlike the ancient Ninevites, who repented at Jonah's preaching, and the Queen of Sheba, who was receptive to Solomon's teaching, the Jewish leaders reject Jesus, who is superior to both prophet and king. So He warns them that unrepentance will eventually result in the demons reinvading in greater numbers. This would make for a condition "worse than the first"—on personal and societal levels.

14. UNFORTUNATELY, GENERATIONAL CURSES APPLY TO CHRISTIANS.

The teaching on generational curses comes from the second commandment, where God prohibits the worship of idols and pronounces a consequence on those who do so: "You shall not bow down to them or worship them; for I, the LORD your God, am a jealous God, punishing the children for the sin of the parents to the third and fourth generation of those who hate me" (Exod. 20:5 NIV). To love God is to "keep his commands" (1 John 5:3 NIV), so to hate God is to disobey Him, "For rebellion is as the sin of witchcraft, and stubbornness is as wickedness and idolatry" (1 Sam. 15:23, author's translation from Hebrew).

---

with the house of Israel and the house of Judah, not like the covenant that I made with their fathers on the day when I took them by the hand to bring them out of the land of Egypt. . . . I will put my law within them, and I will write it on their hearts" (Jer. 31:31–33). Coincidentally, the promised outpouring of the Holy Spirit occurring on the day of Pentecost signified the inauguration of the New Covenant with the "Lawgiver" Himself indwelling the believer (Acts 1:8; 2:1–8).

Those who oppose the concept of generational curses believe Jesus redeemed us from all curses: "Christ redeemed us from the curse of the law by becoming a curse for us" (Gal. 3:13). However, the next verse specifies the result God had in mind: atonement (v. 14). Also, while these proponents make exception for physical death, they gloss over the fact that we still suffer Adam and Eve's curses of work stress and labor pains (Gen. 3:15–19).

Additionally, the New Testament still requires us to keep the Ten Commandments—minus the Sabbath day (Col. 2:16–17)—thus, those scriptural consequences still apply to us:

- "Keep yourselves from idols" (1 John 5:21).
- "For the commandments, 'You shall not commit adultery, You shall not murder, You shall not steal, You shall not covet,' and any other commandment, are summed up in this word: 'You shall love your neighbor as yourself'" (Rom. 13:9).

Moreover, the New Testament reinforces the concepts of curses and blessings by re-emphasizing the fifth commandment: "'Honor your father and mother'—which is the first commandment with a promise—'so that it may go well with you and that you may enjoy long life on the earth'" (Eph. 6:2–3 NIV). Notice the promise implies the curse of a shorter, less qualitative life if we unjustly disobey this commandment.

Furthermore, the matter of generational curses shouldn't mystify us. It falls in line with the idea of original sin—our first parents (Adam and Eve) sinned; now all of us do! The root word in "genetics" and "generational" is *gene*. Unfortunately, our behavior somehow affects our genes, codes our genetics, and impacts our generational offspring.

Surprisingly, science confirms this through epigenetics. Listen to findings from these two neuropsychologists:

1. Dr. Jes Montgomery explains, "[Epigenetics validates] that environment markedly affects our gene expressions and the ways we function and behave."[29]

2. Dr. Tim Jennings elaborates, "The choices we make—the foods that we eat, the things that we watch—can affect how the DNA is expressed. When we have kids, we pass on the sequence to them. So if we become addicted to stuff, we can pass along to our children gene instructions that make them more vulnerable to addictions."[30]

Dr. C. Fred Dickason validates this sobering news when he attests, "I have found this avenue of ancestral involvement to be the chief cause of demonization. Well over 95 percent of more than 400 persons I have contacted in my counseling ministry have been demonized because of their ancestors' involvement in occult and demonic activities."[31]

The good news is epigenetic study also teaches that gene corruption can be reversed by us making better choices. Of course, scientists are still catching up to truths God already revealed over 3,000 years ago. For example, He corrected

29. Jeremy Wiles, "Science Confirms Bible on Generational Curses," Conquer Series, June 22, 2022, https://conquerseries.com/science-confirms-bible-on-generational-curses.

30. Wiles, "Science Confirms Bible on Generational Curses."

31. Dickason, *Demon Possession & the Christian*, 221.

the Israelites when they sought to blame their behavior on their parents (Ezek. 18:2–4). To remove excuses, He shared a story: "Suppose [a violent] son has a son who sees all the sins his father commits, and though he sees them, he does not do such things. . . . He will not die for his father's sin; he will surely live" (18:14, 17 NIV).

It typically takes three to four generations before family members recognize the historical patterns of destructive behavior and realize the need to repent. This is the reason God ends the second commandment with the better option: "But I lavish unfailing love for a thousand generations on those who love me and obey my commands" (Exod. 20:6 NLT).

Let me share a sobering example of a generational curse. My phone rang around 2:00 a.m. It was a church member, Kim, who was babysitting overnight at her home for another family from her small group Bible study. In the middle of the night, Kim was awakened by a mysterious bumping sound. She followed the sounds to the guest bedroom where the family's child was sleeping. When she flipped on the light, the little girl was contorted backward and convulsing against the wall. She called the girl's name several times, the child awoke, and the behavior stopped. At this point, I was now on the phone.

I directed Kim to read aloud Psalm 91 and then pray God's peace over the child. As soon as she began to read the psalm, the little girl started contorting and convulsing again. Before we could address it, Kim suddenly heard bumping coming from the adjacent room where her two-year-old son sleeps. She ran into his room and flipped on the light. Surprisingly, he was emulating the behavior of the little girl. The two children were not biologically related, and Kim had never experienced her son suffering this phenomenon.

After she called his name a few times, he paused, stepped out of the bed, then stood before her. He had a dark, confronting demeanor well beyond the age of a child. Kim panicked. I directed her to place the phone on speaker mode. Sensing this was a generational spirit, I addressed the demons possibly afflicting the boy through the doorway of his mother's and/or father's bloodlines. When I addressed Kim's bloodline, nothing happened. However, as soon as I did the same for his father's bloodline, the boy's head twitched, his pupils flew to the corners of his eyes, and he began to turn in circles while menacingly staring at his mother. After a period of prayer for both children, the incidents subsided.

Later that morning, the parents returned for their daughter, and Kim explained the whole ordeal. However, she was shocked when one of the parents nonchalantly replied, "Oh, this has been happening in our family for several generations." Sadly, they dismissed the possibility of this condition being spiritual, because they didn't believe evil spirits could attack Christians—especially children. However, in Satan's spiritual war against God, he doesn't consider anyone off-limits, even children.

15. UNFORTUNATELY, SATAN CAN ATTACK CHRISTIANS.

Many teach that evil spirits cannot attack believers based on 1 John 5:18–19: "We know that anyone born of God does not continue to sin, but the one born of God preserves him, and the evil one cannot touch him. We know we are from God, and the whole world reclines[32] with[33] the evil one" (author's translation from Greek). The Greek verb translated "touch"[34] also means "to grasp, cling to, or hold on to." Thus, Satan cannot claim us—we're no longer members of his kingdom.

Here are two occasions where touch emphasizes affection:

1. when the religious leaders despise Jesus for allowing a repentant woman to caress and kiss His feet while washing them with her tears and wiping them with her hair (Luke 7:36–39);[35] and

2. when Jesus prevents Mary from trying to embrace Him after His resurrection (John 20:17).

When you combine these concepts, a disturbing picture develops of unbelievers reclining with Satan as he's being affectionate with them.

Thus, the Apostle John is teaching in 1 John 5:18 that true believers no longer make a lifestyle of sin. As a result, Christ safeguards their sincere commitment to Him (1 Cor. 10:13; Col. 1:22; Jude 24); so Satan no longer engages in an illicit relationship with them—it would be incompatible with their profession of faith. This reality is also confirmed by the abrupt ending of 1 John: "Keep yourselves from idols" (5:21), which are essentially demons (Deut. 32:17; 1 Cor. 10:19–20; Rev. 9:20).

Therefore, 1 John 5:18 doesn't exempt Christians from spiritual warfare. This is also validated by the Bible com-

32. Greek: κεῖμαι (keimai), to lie down or be in a set or relaxed position (DANK, 3632).

33. Greek: ἐν (en), "in" or "with," given the context (DANK, 2196).

34. Greek: ἅπτω (haptō), to touch or have sexual relations [1 Cor. 7:1] (DANK, 861).

35. The exact form is used only here.

manding us—on three separate occasions—to put on the full armor of God (Rom. 13:12; Eph. 6:11–13; 1 Thess. 5:8). Even stronger, the Bible defines the Christian life as waging war against demons (2 Cor. 10:3; 1 Tim. 1:18).[36] As a matter of fact, two of the most prominent Apostles were demonically attacked. Surprisingly, Jesus didn't rebuke the devil when he requested to test Peter's faith. Instead, He warned Peter to be strong (Luke 22:31–32). Also, God allowed a demon to physically torment Paul to lessen the pride he developed due to his miraculous experiences (2 Cor. 12:7–8).

These examples verify that on occasion God allows Satan to tempt, trouble, and torment us. Yet He supplies us with everything we need to overcome or endure the battle (1 Cor. 10:13; 2 Cor. 4:8–9; 12:9). However, believers are promised special protection during the process of expelling demons (Luke 10:19).

Here's a modern-day example. A college student from another state, Douglas, contacted me after obtaining my information from a counseling agency. He was seeing a therapist to address a number of unresolved childhood traumas. After a series of sessions, the counselor, who happened to be a Christian, believed Douglas's personal afflictions were the result of something sinister.

One night, upon arriving at his dorm room, Douglas sensed a presence. He looked around, saw nothing, then looked up. From a dot on his ceiling, a dark face emerged, then massive horns appeared, followed by broad shoulders. He remained frozen in fear as a shadow creature of immense

---

36. Greek: στρατεύω (*strateuó*), "of a Christian worker *resist evil, struggle against evil forces*" (Friberg, 25041).

size looked down on him. Intuitively, Douglas sensed this to be the evil spirit who had tormented him all his life. He stared at the demon and gasped, "I know you." After a short pause, it replied, "And I know . . . you."

Douglas tried to scream, but there was no sound. He attempted to move but couldn't. Eventually, he was able to mutter for the demon to go away in the Name of Jesus, but nothing happened, because he had no biblical authority as a non-Christian. To further intimidate Douglas, the demon held him captive in that room, towering over him with its imposing presence, revealing itself as the source of his troubles, and striving to deceive him into thinking it had ultimate control of his life.

After a moment that felt like an eternity, the demon slowly backed out of the ceiling. Terrified, Douglas sprinted to a close friend's dorm room, crying uncontrollably. The next day, he shared the frightening encounter with his therapist, who secretly prayed for him. After suffering a few more months from hauntings and torments, he decided to give his life to Christ. However, the demonic attacks did not stop.

Searching for relief, a friend introduced him to a pastor who was trained in spiritual warfare. They met privately, and when the pastor began to pray for him, a demon surfaced within Douglas. As a battle raged for his mind, he agonized that his skull felt like it was being pulled apart. Eventually, the evil spirit was expelled, and Douglas finally experienced freedom from the demon who had afflicted him since his childhood.

You may be thinking, *If he was demonized, was he really a Christian?* This is a perfect transition into the next chapter, "Can Christians Be Demonized?"

7

CAN CHRISTIANS BE DEMONIZED?

Ancient records share the account of a young rabbi who was curious about the existence of demons. He performed an experiment and "saw the demons and was harmed."[1] He was healed only after a group of rabbis pleaded for God's mercy on his behalf.[2]

When the modern world entered the industrial revolution, it rationalized Satan out of existence. However, as the postmodern world explores practices long forbidden by the Bible, spiritual outcomes are forcing the church to realize the devil was among us all along.

The evil one has been active in this world since the third chapter of the Bible. Demonization is just one of his spiritual warfare tactics. The Old Testament doesn't give us many examples of this, but there are two accepted cases. The first is of King Saul, who became demonized after the Spirit of God departed from him due to his disobedience (1 Sam. 16:14–23).

1. BT, Berakhot 6a.6.
2. BT, Berakhot 6a.6.

The second is of a demon[3] who visited and became "a lying spirit in the mouth" of the false prophets. In turn, they enticed wicked King Ahab to launch a forbidden war that resulted in his death on the battlefield (1 Kings 22:22).

Although the Gospels present numerous cases of demonization, they occur *before* the promised indwelling of the Holy Spirit fulfilled on the first Pentecost after the death, resurrection, and ascension of Christ. Therefore, is it possible for New Covenant believers, who are indwelled by the Holy Spirit, to be demonized? For an informed answer, we need to explore

1. ancient Jewish history *before*, *during*, and *after* Christ;
2. New Testament Scriptures after the indwelling of the Holy Spirit;
3. analyses from recognized scholars;
4. accounts from the early church;
5. excerpts from later church history; and
6. testimonies from modern pastors.

DEMONIZATION *BEFORE* CHRIST

Since the Old Testament is scarce on the subject of demonization, we must rely on ancient literature to accurately reconstruct Jewish beliefs about demons in the centuries *before* Christ.[4]

3. First Kings 22:22 actually says "spirit," but with New Testament hindsight, we know this to be a demon, since (1) the godly Prophet Micaiah told King Ahab not to make war (1 Kings 22:15–17); (2) the spirit enticed the king to oppose God's will—the role of a devil (adversary); and (3) it is out of character for a holy angel to serve as a deceiver.

4. Graham H. Twelftree, *Jesus the Exorcist: A Contribution to the Study of the Historical Jesus* (Peabody, MA: Hendrickson, 1993). He states, "In 1 Enoch,

Ancient Jews viewed demons as harmful and wicked, so they exhausted much effort to ward off demonic presence—especially from their homes.[5] We even find guidance about haunted houses, places, and fields.[6] In artwork, demons are typically depicted with horns and bodies composed of human and animal features. Wings were also added to identify them as supernatural beings.[7] One ancient source describes how demons manifested: "You bark like dogs, you grunt like pigs, you hiss like snakes . . . you make yourselves visible . . . in bad dreams, in a hateful shape."[8]

Also, expelling demons was a popular practice among Jewish religious leaders and common people alike. Advice was passed down from teacher to student—even parent to child.[9]

Perhaps a more fascinating discovery took place in the mid-1900s when archaeologists unearthed the Dead Sea Scrolls.[10]

Tobit, Jubilees, Qumran scrolls, Josephus, Philo of Alexandria, Pseudo-Philo's Liber Antiquitatim Biblicarum (LAB), the magical papyri, Lucian of Samosata, Apollonius of Tyana and rabbinic literature can, with varying degrees of ease and reliability, be used to provide material to reconstruct first century understandings of spirits, demons, possessions, magic, healing, healers, exorcisms and exorcists" (16–17). He adds, "First century Palestinians were most probably well aware of, and practiced forms of exorcism that are represented in the ancient Babylonian and Egyptian texts" (226). See also Josephus, *Antiquities of the Jews* 2, 5, 8, 45–48, where Josephus documents occurrences of possession and exorcism.

5. Bohak, "Expelling Demons and Attracting Demons in Jewish Magical Texts," 171. He adds, "The evidence for this comes in the form of incantation bowls, that is, standard earthenware bowls on the inside of which were written elaborate spells and adjurations" (171).

6. BT, Berakhot 3b.9.

7. Rüdiger Schmitt, "Demons, Demonology," in *The Encyclopedia of the Bible and Its Reception*, vol. 6 of *Dabbesheth—Dreams and Dream Interpretation* (Berlin: de Gruyter, 2012), 537.

8. Bohak, "Expelling Demons and Attracting Demons in Jewish Magical Texts," 179.

9. Bohak, "Jewish Exorcisms Before and After the Destruction of the Second Temple," 299.

10. The discovery was in the Qumran Caves located in modern-day West Bank in Israel.

Among them, they found the "Psalms Scroll." It claims King David wrote four psalms to be specifically spoken over the demonized.[11] These psalms are believed to be among the scrolls recovered there. The first of the four psalms is deteriorated and unreadable. The second is in good condition but still hard to read. The third is in great condition—a quotation of interest is when the demon Resheph is mocked for having "horns of sand." The fourth and last one is well preserved and the only one found in the Bible: Psalm 91.[12]

Ancient Jews understood Psalm 91 to offer protection from demons—especially during the ministry of expelling them.[13] Consider the ancient Aramaic translation (*targum*) of this psalm.[14] To stay on topic, we'll focus on only verses 5–10, where King David instructs his son Solomon:

New International Version	Aramaic Targum[15]
You will not fear the terror of night, nor the arrow that flies by day, (v. 5)	You will not be afraid of the terror *of the demons* that go about in the night, nor of the arrow *of the angel of death* that he shoots in the daytime,

11. Florentino García Martínez and Eibert J. C. Tigchelaar, *The Dead Sea Scrolls Study Edition*, vol. 2 (Leiden, the Netherlands: Brill, 1998), 1178–79 (11Q5 [or 11QPsa] 27:9–10). Also, it appears the historian gave David credit for other psalms written under his kingship.

12. Martínez and Tigchelaar, *Dead Sea Scrolls*, 1178–79.

13. In Jewish theology, this applied to physical as well as spiritual war because they believed attacks from those outside the covenant community were ultimately influenced by demons, since they were battling against the "children of darkness."

14. For analysis involving Hebrew, Greek, and other linguistic insights into Psalm 91, I recommend Heiser, *Demons*, 34–36, 54–56, 211.

15. Craig A. Evans, "Jesus and Psalm 91 in Light of the Exorcism Scrolls," in *Celebrating the Dead Sea Scrolls*, ed. Peter W. Flint, Jean Duhaime, and Kyung S. Baek (Leiden, the Netherlands: Brill, 2012), 548–49. Also, see page 554, where Dr. Evans assesses a pre-Christ dating for the Aramaic Targum: "The appearance of Psalm 91 in the Matthean and Lukan versions of the temptation of Jesus is but one indication of many that the demonological orientation of this particular psalm in the Psalms Targum derives from early, probably intertestamental tradition. The exorcistic psalms of 11Q11 provide important, early attestation of a tradition that comes to expression in interesting ways in the life and teaching of Jesus."

New International Version	Aramaic Targum
nor the pestilence that stalks in the darkness, nor the plague that destroys at midday. (v. 6)	nor *of the death* that goes about in the darkness, nor of the company *of demons* that destroy at noon.
A thousand may fall at your side, ten thousand at your right hand, but it will not come near you. (v. 7)	*You will call to remembrance the Holy Name,* and a thousand will fall at your left side, and ten thousand at your right hand; (but) *they* will not come near you *to do harm.*
You will only observe with your eyes and see the punishment of the wicked. (v. 8)	You will only look with your eyes, and you will see how the wicked are being destroyed.
If you say, "The LORD is my refuge," and you make the Most High your dwelling, (v. 9)	*Solomon answered,*[16] and this is what he said: "Because you, O Lord, are my refuge, in the most high dwelling place you have set the house of your [dwelling]."[17]
no harm will overtake you, no disaster will come near your tent. (v. 10)	*The Lord of the World responded, and this is what he said:* "No *evil* shall befall you, and *no plague or demons* shall come near your tent."

These four points stand out:

1. Demons are considered the main source of misfortune;
2. The "angel of death" is associated with demons;[18]
3. Calling on the Name of the Lord activates the powers of protection; and
4. Verse 7 implies hordes of demons as supported by rabbinic literature: "Each and every one of us has a

---

16. The insertion of Solomon's name in verse 9 is likely due to ancient sources mentioning him as devising successful methods to expel demons (Josephus, *Antiquities of the Jews* 8.45).

17. Original is *shekinah*.

18. See Evans, "Jesus and Psalm 91," 549. He also references Targum Psalm 89:32 [Eng. 89:33], where the wicked are struck down in Gehenna by the angel of death and "demons number among the allies of the angel of death."

thousand demons to his left and ten thousand to his right. God protects man from these demons, as it says in the verse: 'A thousand may fall at your side, and ten thousand at your right hand.'"[19]

Some scholars debate the early date for the Targum. However, the Greek Septuagint, written approximately 300 years before Christ, translates Psalm 91:5–6 as follows:

> You shall not be afraid
>> of the terror by night,
>> of the arrow flying by day,
>> of the *evil thing*[20] lurking in darkness,
>> of the destruction and *demon* at noonday.
>> (Author's translation from Greek)

Therefore, the Greek Septuagint confirms the ancient belief that this psalm offered protection from evil spirits.

DEMONIZATION *DURING* THE TIME OF CHRIST

As the Bible confirms, Jews expelled demons *before and during* the time of Christ (Matt. 12:27; Luke 11:19). However, they naturally expected the prophesied Savior to do so on an even greater scale since He was to come from the lineage of King David (Matt. 1:1). As anticipated, the crowds marveled when Jesus expelled demons, because He did so on a level they had never witnessed. Jesus differed from all those

---

19. BT, Berakhot 6a.
20. Greek: πρᾶγμα (*pragma*), "thing, matter; of bad activity" (DANK, 5283); thus, the adjective "evil."

before Him because He did not consult the religious leaders for guidance, rely on rituals or relics, or quote Scripture. He didn't even refer to Psalm 91, because He is its true author and the God of that promise (John 1:1). He simply commanded demons to leave, and they left.

Jesus expelled demons to demonstrate darkness being dispelled by the light. This is why exorcism was utilized as a central action of the Gospels. In his book *Jesus the Exorcist*, Bible scholar Dr. Graham H. Twelftree declares, "To sketch a picture of the historical Jesus without significant reference to his ministry of exorcism is to produce a distortion of the evidence."[21] Jesus's exorcisms weren't efforts to prepare for His kingdom "but were themselves the kingdom of God in operation."[22] Jesus said, "But if I drive out demons by the finger of God, then the kingdom of God has come upon you" (Luke 11:20 NIV; see also Matt. 12:28).

DEMONIZATION *AFTER* THE TIME OF CHRIST (PERIOD OF THE APOSTLES)

During His ministry, Jesus delegated the duties of expelling demons to His disciples (Matt. 10:1, 8; Mark 3:14–15; Luke 10:1, 17). Consistent with the culture, Christians *during and after* Jesus understood this to be a general ability among all His followers (Matt. 7:22; Mark 9:38–39; Luke 9:49–50; Acts 19:13–15).

Before God the Son ascended back to heaven, He prayed to God the Father, "I do not ask that you take them out of the world, but that you keep them from the evil one" (John

---

21. Twelftree, *Jesus the Exorcist*, 225.
22. Twelftree, *Jesus the Exorcist*, 218.

17:15). Jesus knew Satan would remain active after His departure. Thus, His followers would need protection from demons. The New Testament writers knew this too. Even after the promised indwelling of the Holy Spirit, every New Testament author (but not every book) discusses the dangers of evil spirits. As theologian Dr. Eric Sorensen affirms, "Demonology attests to the need for salvation [from sin] and deliverance from Satan, which the [New Testament] authors collectively interpret as occurring through Christ's ministry, death, and resurrection."[23]

Regarding the continual need for the ministry of expelling demons, Dr. Millard J. Erickson affirms, "There is no reason to believe [demonizations] are restricted to the past. . . . The Christian should be alert to the possibility of [demonization] occurring today."[24]

I reviewed all the main arguments against Christians being demonized.[25] As unsettling as it may be, there's no Scripture in the New Testament that explicitly states a Christian cannot be demonized. The most common argument against it is that God and Satan cannot dwell in the same place. However, that argument is incorrect based on these two scriptural truths: (1) there are examples of Satan making regular trips

23. Eric Sorensen, "Demons, Demonology," in *The Encyclopedia of the Bible and Its Reception*, vol. 6 of *Dabbesheth—Dreams and Dream Interpretation* (Berlin: de Gruyter, 2012), 541. In brackets, I spelled out "New Testament" and added "from sin" for clarity.

24. Millard J. Erickson, *Christian Theology* (Grand Rapids: Baker Books, 1985), 450. Also, brackets indicate where I updated his original word *demon-possession* with *demonization*.

25. Dr. C. Fred Dickason gives sound analysis (exegesis) of biblical arguments for and against Christians becoming demonized. Thus, I recommend a review of pages 81–127 of Dickason, *Demon Possession & the Christian*. From my perspective, scriptural certainty is provided by the inclusion of church history on the subject, which will be introduced later in this chapter.

to heaven to accuse people before God, so both were present in the same place (Job 1:6; 2:1; Zech. 3:1–3); and (2) God is all-present, so He is in the midst of evil everywhere (Jer. 23:24; Eph. 4:10).

To this, Dr. Charles C. Ryrie adds:

> The argument against a believer being able to be demon[ized] is . . . since the Spirit indwells the believer, it is impossible for Satan or demons also to indwell and thus possess the believer at the same time. But do not the Spirit and the flesh war within the believer? (Gal. 5:16–17) If it be argued that the old man has been judged (Rom. 6:6), it may also be pointed out that Satan has been judged too (John 12:31). So if Spirit and flesh, the new and old, can be present within the believer at the same time, why cannot the Spirit and Satan (or demons)?[26]

Even renowned Bible scholar and archaeologist Dr. Merrill F. Unger officially reversed his position and admitted that "it was based on the assumption that an evil spirit could not indwell the redeemed body together with the Holy Spirit," and "it was inferred, since Scripture does not clearly settle the question."[27] This change in position occurred "after numbers of letters and reports of cases of demon invasion of believers have come to me from missionaries in various parts of the world."[28] Some accounts included "cases of

---

26. Charles C. Ryrie, *Basic Theology* (Chicago: Victor, 1988), 167. I updated "demon-possessed" with "demonized."

27. Merrill F. Unger, *Demons in the World Today* (Wheaton: Tyndale, 1971), 116–17.

28. Merrill F. Unger, *What Demons Can Do to Saints* (Chicago: Moody, 1977), 59–60.

repossession among converts."[29] Dr. Unger also reiterates what I claim at the beginning of this section: "The truth of the matter is that the Scriptures nowhere plainly state that a true believer cannot be invaded by Satan or his demons."[30]

Perhaps the strongest New Testament argument that a Christian can be demonized is found in Acts 5:3: "Peter said, 'Ananias, why has Satan filled your heart to lie to the Holy Spirit and to keep back for yourself part of the proceeds of the land?'" The Greek word translated "filled"[31] is the same one used of a believer being "filled with the Holy Spirit" (Eph. 5:18 NLT). Ananias was a believer associated with the church in Jerusalem (Acts 2:44–45; 5:1–2). Believers were selling their land and possessions to meet the common needs of the persecuted church. Ananias wanted to be socially recognized for being self-sacrificial, but he secretly withheld a portion of his donation for selfish gain. His intent was to benefit from the sacrifices of others while keeping his own hidden stash. In this case, the Apostle Peter confronts him for lying. Thus, this could be an example of manipulation serving as a doorway to demonization.

Besides manipulation, there are other motives and emotions considered demonic, including anger, jealousy, and selfish ambition. Regarding ungodly anger, the Bible warns, "Be angry, but do not sin; do not let the sun go down upon your wrath nor give a room to the devil" (Eph. 4:26–27, author's translation from Greek). One of the meanings for the Greek word for "room" is "to denote a specific and defined area."[32]

29. Unger, *Demons in the World Today*, 117.
30. Unger, *What Demons Can Do to Saints*, 59.
31. Greek: πληρόω (*plēróō*), "filled" (DANK, 5183).
32. Greek: τόπος (*topos*), "room or place" (Friberg, 26900).

For the believer, what "specific or defined area" would that be if not within the body?

Next, there is, surprisingly, an emotion worse than anger. "Anger is cruel, and wrath is like a flood, but jealousy is even more dangerous" (Prov. 27:4 NLT). The Bible couples it with selfish ambition and refers to Satan as the source of both:

> But if you are bitterly jealous and there is selfish ambition in your heart, don't cover up the truth with boasting and lying. For jealousy and selfishness are not God's kind of wisdom. Such things are earthly, unspiritual, and demonic. For wherever there is jealousy and selfish ambition, there you will find disorder and evil of every kind. (James 3:14–16 NLT)

This is the only place in the New Testament the Greek word for "demonic" is used. It is defined as "resembling or proceeding from an evil spirit, demon-like."[33] Both jealousy and selfish ambition foster an environment where "evil of every kind" exists.

So diabolical are these four motives and emotions that, if unchecked, they can lead to murder.

1. *Manipulation:* Jesus called Satan a "liar" and "murderer" (John 8:44).
2. *Anger:* Jesus warns of anger's link to potential murder (Matt. 5:21–22).

---

33. Greek: δαιμονιώδης (*daimoniōdēs*), "demonic, demon-like" (Joseph Thayer, *A Greek-English Lexicon of the New Testament* [abridged and revised Thayer Lexicon] [Ontario: Online Bible Foundation, 1997], 1193; hereafter Thayer).

3. *Jealousy:* Cain murdered Abel due to God blessing Abel's offerings but not his (Gen. 4:4–8).

4. *Selfish ambition:* King Herod murdered all the boys in Bethlehem who were two years old or younger because he believed Jesus's birth was an eventual threat to his throne (Matt. 2:16).[34]

If a person still doesn't believe a Christian can be demonized—even after exhibiting these sinister behaviors—let's consider some accounts from church history.

DEMONIZATION IN THE EARLY CHURCH

What did early church leaders think about the possibility of Christians being demonized? Also, why is church history important on this topic? The Bible proclaims that believers triumph over Satan "by the blood of the Lamb and by the word of their testimony" (Rev. 12:11). Thayer's Greek Lexicon defines the word *testimony* as "in an historical sense, of the testimony of an historian."[35] Thus, the writings of the early church leaders below are considered historical accounts of their encounters and teachings regarding demonized Christians.

Tertullian (c. AD 155–220, early Christian theologian) shares the case of a Christian woman becoming demonized as a warning to avoid unwholesome places of entertainment:

34. Two other examples of kings are (1) Abimelech killed 70 of his brothers to prevent them from competing with his desire to rule in place of his father (Judg. 9:1–5); and (2) Saul tried multiple times to assassinate David, who was prophesied and anointed to take his place due to sin (1 Sam. 18:11, 17, 21; 19:1, 10–11, 15, 20–22; 23:15; 26:2).

35. Greek: μαρτυρία (*marturia*), "testimony" (Thayer, 3329).

What sort of behavior is it to go from the assembly of God to the assembly of the Devil, from sky to sty, as the saying goes? . . . To cheer a gladiator with the same lips with which you have said "Amen" over the Most Holy? . . . Why, then, should such people [Christians] not also be susceptible to demoniac possession? For we have the case of that woman—the Lord is witness—who went to the theater [to watch people be maimed and murdered] and returned home having a demon. So, when in the course of exorcism the unclean spirit was hard pressed with the accusation that he had dared to seize a *woman who believed*, he answered boldly: "I was fully justified in doing so, for I found her in my own domain."[36]

Next, the *Epistle of Barnabas* (c. late first century) speaks to the extent of our spiritual condition before coming to faith in Christ: "Before we believed in God, the habitation of our heart . . . was full of idolatry, and was the house of demons through doing things which were contrary to God."[37] Consistently, ancient Jews and early Christians, respectively, label unbelievers "children of darkness"[38] and "children of the devil" (1 John 3:10; see also Eph. 2:3). While all people are created in the image of God, the Bible doesn't consider people "children of God" until they submit to the Lordship of Jesus Christ (John 1:12; Gal. 3:26). Also, since Satan is "the god of this world" (2 Cor. 4:4), an idol can include any unbiblical belief or behavior promoted in the place of the true God. For example:

36. Tertullian, *On the Spectacles [or Shows] (De Spectaculis)*, 25, 26.
37. *Epistle of Barnabas* 16.7.
38. Qumran Scrolls sections I and III.

1. Any devotion to an idol is actually offered to a demon (Deut. 32:17; 1 Cor. 10:19–20).
2. Any belief that excludes Jesus as the Christ and denies He is the only means to eternal life is idolatry (1 John 4:1–2; 5:12, 21).[39]
3. Sex outside a monogamous, heterosexual marriage is also considered idolatry; the Greek construction of Colossians 3:5 applies this to all aspects of forbidden sexuality (fornication, defilement, lust, evil desire, and insatiability).
4. Willful disobedience is equated to idol worship (1 Sam. 15:23).

What bearing does this have on Christians being demonized? The concept of the unbeliever's body being the temple of idols (demons) is a natural transition into the early Christian practice of expelling demons from new converts:

1. Hippolytus (c. AD 170–235, Bishop of Rome): "If any man is possessed with demons, he shall not be admitted as a [student][40] until he is cleansed."[41]
2. Cyril (c. AD 376–444, Bishop of Jerusalem): "Without exorcisms the soul cannot be purified."[42]

39. See I. Howard Marshall, *The Epistles of John* (Grand Rapids: Eerdmans, 1978). Dr. Marshall comments on the abrupt ending and command "do not worship idols" in 1 John 5:21: "John urges his readers to have nothing to do with false ideas of God and the sins that go with them" (256).
40. Original word is *bearer*.
41. Hippolytus, *Apostolic Tradition* 16.8. See also chaps. 17–18, where the context indicates this "someone" is a new convert. For example, chap. 18 instructs, "Catechumen [Latin for "one who is being instructed"] will hear the word for three years."
42. Philip Schaff and Henry Wace, eds., *Procatechesis*, in *Nicene and Post-Nicene Fathers, Second Series*, vol. 7 (Buffalo: Christian Literature Publishing Co., 1894), https://www.newadvent.org/fathers/310100.htm.

This is why Hippolytus further instructs:

> Then from the time that they are separated from the other [new students],[43] hands shall be laid upon them daily in exorcism and, as the day of their baptism draws near, the bishop himself shall exorcise each one of them that he may be personally assured of their purity. Then, if there is any of them who is not good or pure, he shall be put aside as not having heard the word in faith;[44] for it is never possible for the [demon][45] to be concealed.[46]

Let's pause for a moment to ponder these early Christian teachings:

1. Unbelievers potentially have demons *before* they submit to Christ.
2. New converts must be screened for demons *after* they submit to Christ.
3. The ministry of expelling demons is primarily for the well-being of the believer because it breaks demonic ties that can interfere with effective discipleship.[47]

---

43. Original word is *catechumen* (Latin).

44. For clarity, this phrase is in relation to post-conversion Bible training as confirmed by Hippolytus, *Apostolic Tradition* 18:1: "When the teacher finishes his instruction, the catechumens [students] will pray by themselves, separate from the faithful." As with all Christians, Bible learning reveals more attitudes and behaviors from which we must repent.

45. Original word is *alien*, as in a "foreign spirit."

46. Hippolytus, *Apostolic Tradition* 20.3–4.

47. Purity is an act of repentance (2 Cor. 11:2–3; 1 Tim. 5:22; James 4:8; 1 John 3:3).

For clarity, early church pastors eventually delayed baptisms to ensure new converts were properly instructed on biblical belief and behavior due to the Gospel spreading into pagan territories. Nevertheless, early Christians remained consistent with ancient Jews who considered baptism a part of the process of cleansing oneself from the impurity of idols (demons).[48]

Early church historians bore witness to demonized Christians. More importantly, they understood that this spiritual condition did *not* contradict the New Testament.

DEMONIZATION IN LATER CHURCH HISTORY

As history progressed, evil persisted. Regarding Judaism, Dr. Gideon Bohak declares the period between late antiquity and medieval times (AD 200–1400) "was full of demons."[49] This is evidenced by archaeology and literature. As a rule, ancient Jews believed no one was exempt from demonic attacks.[50] Yet the ancient answer remained the same for a victim afflicted by evil spirits: turn to God for help.[51] Eventually, modern thinkers considered ancient viewpoints to be outdated. This is why most books today on rabbinic Judaism rarely discuss demons.[52]

As a parallel to that time period, the church continued in its endeavors to confront the darkness. Before Jesus was crucified, He prayed His church would be one just as He and

---

48. BT, Sotah 12b.2.
49. Bohak, "Conceptualizing Demons in Late Antique Judaism," 111.
50. Bohak, "Conceptualizing Demons in Late Antique Judaism," 129–30. A few very devout rabbis were considered an exception to this rule.
51. Bohak, "Conceptualizing Demons in Late Antique Judaism," 111.
52. Bohak, "Conceptualizing Demons in Late Antique Judaism," 112.

the Father are one (John 17:22). Christians were unified as one universal[53] church for over 1,000 years. However, in AD 1054, the first church split called the "Great Schism" took place between the Eastern and Western sects of the universal church.

Then nearly 500 years later in AD 1517, the second church split known as the "Protestant Reformation" occurred in the Western universal church (later known in title as the "Roman Catholic Church"). That split is where most mainline European and American denominations trace their origins.

The bit of history above will help us to appreciate the examples below of exorcisms continuing before and after the Reformation. As a matter of fact, the two longest-standing churches (Roman Catholic and Eastern Orthodox) continue the practice of expelling demons.[54]

Consider also these recorded events:

1. From AD 1090 to 1179, actual accounts of demonization significantly increased along with instructions on how to expel demons.[55]

2. In the 1500s, among numerous reports, one circulated about a group of girls freed from demons

---

53. The actual word is *catholic*. It stems from Greek and Latin meaning "universal."

54. William S. Chavez, "Modern Practice, Archaic Ritual: Catholic Exorcism in America," *Religions* 12, no. 10 (September 2021): https://www.mdpi.com/2077-1444/12/10/811; George C. Papademetriou, "Exorcism in the Orthodox Church," Greek Orthodox Archdiocese of America, September 3, 1990, https://www.goarch.org/-/exorcism-in-the-orthodox-church.

55. Nancy Caciola, "Exorcism," in *Encyclopedia of Religion*, 2nd ed. (Detroit: Macmillan Reference, 2005), 2929.

summoned by their father, who was offended they converted to Christianity from Judaism.[56]

3. In 1608, the manual *Compendium Maleficarum* (Latin for "compilation of evil deeds") was written and included four signs of extreme demonization—bodily contortions, levitation, supernatural strength, and speaking in languages never learned by the victim (it is still referenced by some today).[57]

Forging ahead:

1. In the late 1800s, Henry Drummond, an evangelist who served under the famous D. L. Moody, admitted being demonized with psychic abilities he never renounced after his conversion. "He was able to bring the large audiences at Moody's meetings under his hypnotic influence . . . [so] he pleaded with the Lord to take them away . . . and was completely delivered."[58]

2. In 1949, a 13-year-old boy, referred to as "Roland Doe," was demonized after using a Ouija board to consult his aunt who recently died. It took 20 separate sessions to expel all the demons. This true story inspired the 1973 film *The Exorcist*.[59]

3. In 1973, Frank Hammond, a graduate of Baylor University and Southwestern Baptist Theological

56. Caciola, "Exorcism," 2931.

57. Joseph Laycock, "Demons, Demonology," in *The Encyclopedia of the Bible and Its Reception*, vol. 6 of *Dabḥesheth—Dreams and Dream Interpretation* (Berlin: de Gruyter, 2012), 566.

58. Kurt Koch, *Occult Bondage and Deliverance* (Grand Rapids: Kregel, 1970), 56.

59. William DeLong, "Inside the Harrowing Exorcism of Roland Doe, the True Story Behind 'The Exorcist,'" *All That's Interesting*, October 5, 2021, https://allthatsinteresting.com/roland-doe-the-exorcist-true-story.

Seminary, and his wife (Ida Mae) published "Pigs in the Parlor," an instruction manual on expelling demons.

Moving into our modern day:

1. From 1975 to 1987, Dr. C. Fred Dickason, professor emeritus of theology at Moody Bible Institute, counseled numerous clients and concluded, "I have encountered at least four hundred genuine believers who were actually inhabited by demons. . . . I found that most of them were accurate in their suspicions that they were being demonically harassed."[60]

2. In 1981, Dr. Rodney Hogue (author, pastor, and adjunct professor), while a doctoral student at Southwestern Baptist Theological Seminary, admitted to being a "Christian with a demon." As the son of a pastor, he did not believe Christians could be demonized until God revealed that he was. He commanded the evil spirit to depart from him in the Name of Jesus, and to his surprise, he felt a presence leave his body.[61]

3. In 2013, Robert Morris (senior pastor of Gateway Church, Dallas, Texas) confessed to tens of thousands of attendees that he was once demonized while serving as an ordained minister, and evil spirits departed from him as the result of repentance, confession, and prayer.[62]

---

60. Dickason, *Demon Possession & the Christian*, 187.
61. Rodney Hogue, "I Was a Christian . . . with a Demon!," *Supernatural Stories*, May 19, 2020, https://www.youtube.com/watch?v=VE3FfhQgDPM.
62. Robert Morris, "Free Indeed Series: Set Free," Gateway Church, Dallas, Texas, January 1, 2014, https://www.gatewaypeople.com/sermons.

4. From 1989 to 2024, I counseled numerous Christians who were shocked to discover their unresolved medical and mental health issues were the result of being demonized.

YOUNG TEEN DEMONIZED WHILE EVANGELIZING

One of my colleagues was stunned by an encounter at his church one Sunday. On the prior Saturday, they had taken their youth group to the town square on Halloween day to share their faith. Some of the youth remembered a group of witches pointing at them, then gathering in a circle. The next day as they were preparing to worship, one of the young ladies began to convulse and growl. At that point, all they knew was to confront the spirit as they had seen on television.

To their surprise, when they asked the spirit how it entered her, it said, "I came forth when the witches prayed against you. I was able to enter her because of her unconfessed sins." They successfully expelled the demon. However, it caused my friend, those teens, and their church leaders to re-evaluate their theological views on Christians being demonized.

HEARTFELT APPEALS FROM A PASTOR AND, IRONICALLY, A PSYCHIATRIST

If my colleague had remained adamant that a Christian cannot be demonized, what condition would that young lady be in today? In this chapter, we reviewed

1. ancient Jewish history *before*, *during*, and *after* Christ;
2. New Testament Scriptures after the indwelling of the Holy Spirit;

3. analyses from recognized scholars;

4. accounts from the early church;

5. excerpts from later church history; and

6. testimonies from modern pastors.

The consensus is that the ministry of expelling demons never ceased and the need for it continues—especially for the well-being of Christians.

In this book, I share cases involving depression, suicidal ideation, mysterious health issues, addictions, even a person with Bible-induced narcolepsy. Most of them claimed to be Christians who were suffering in spiritual battle but found freedom in Christ.

Are we placing believers at a spiritual disadvantage by disregarding the ministry of expelling demons? Have we unknowingly de-emphasized this ministry due to being disconnected from our historical roots?

Ironically, a psychiatrist, Dr. Richard Gallagher, advocates for demonized Christians:

> I've helped clergy from multiple denominations . . . to filter episodes of mental illness . . . from, literally, the devil's work. . . . The same habits that shape what I do as a professor and psychiatrist—open-mindedness, respect for evidence and compassion for suffering people—led me to aid in the work of discerning attacks by what I believe are evil spirits. . . . As I see it, the evidence for [demonization] is like the evidence for George Washington's crossing of the Delaware. In both cases, written historical accounts with numerous sound witnesses testify to their accuracy. . . . *Those who dismiss these cases unwittingly prevent patients from receiving the help*

they desperately require, either by failing to recommend them for psychiatric treatment . . . or by not informing their spiritual ministers that something beyond a mental or other illness seems to be the issue. For any person of science or faith, it should be impossible to turn one's back on a tormented soul.[63]

63. Richard Gallagher, "As a Psychiatrist, I Diagnose Mental Illness. Also, I Help Spot Demon Possession," *Washington Post*, July 1, 2016, emphasis added. Original word in brackets is *possession*.

8

CONFRONTING DEMONS THROUGH REPENTANCE

Fascinating is the word I think of when reflecting on scenarios we explored in my university cross-cultural studies. A missionary mentor shared the story of a mysterious encounter he had after baptizing a tribal leader. As he and his wife prepared to serve abroad in this emerging economy, they were appropriately trained, educated in the language, and carefully immersed in the culture. They were befriended by a tribal leader who served as an ambassador for the village and taught them their customs. After two years, they were able to successfully share the Gospel with him, and he placed his faith in Christ. When the tribal leader shared his decision with the villagers, they rejoiced with him, because they had just discovered a new god to add to their collection of idols.

By all accounts, there were no problems—until he was baptized a few days later. Fear immediately gripped the people, and the tribal leader was disowned and banned from the village. Only after another year of evangelizing those villagers did the missionaries discover why. When the tribal leader was baptized, the local witch doctor sensed intense anger from the other gods and deemed the village to be in danger. Supernaturally, his baptism revealed to their gods that they were all being replaced by the Chief God, Jesus.[1]

REPENTANCE—A HISTORICAL LINK BETWEEN BAPTISM AND SPIRITUAL WARFARE

What makes baptism special? It is effective only if it is "the pledge of a clear conscience toward God" (1 Pet. 3:21 NIV). This is the language of repentance. The word *baptize* simply means "to wash."[2] Ancient homes didn't have bathtubs and shower stalls, so people either drew from or bathed in nearby bodies of water (Exod. 2:5; 2 Kings 5:14). We are most familiar with the ceremonial aspect, yet it was practiced for several centuries before Christ.[3]

When John the Baptist preached, what was his first word? "Repent" (Matt. 3:1–2). People responded by undergoing baptism (3:11). When Jesus began His ministry, what was His first recorded word? "Repent" (4:17). This action is essential to the Christian way of life. It combines the use of two Greek words that mean "change" and "thinking."[4] The noun form (*repentance*) means "the act of changing your mind." Why

1. John 10:33; Col. 1:15–16; 1 John 5:20.
2. Greek: βαπτίζω (*baptizō*).
3. In my discussion with a rabbinic colleague, I learned that the Jews coming out of Egypt baptized themselves to prepare for God's arrival at Mount Sinai (Exod. 19:10–11; 29:4; 30:20; 40:12).
4. Greek: μετανοέω (*meta-noeō*) combines *meta* (change) and *noeō* (thinking).

the mind? The ancients knew it to be the operating system for the body. Therefore, people cannot change in ways that please God unless they align their thinking with biblical truth. This is why the Apostle Paul commands, "Continue to be transformed by the renewal of your mind" (Rom. 12:2, author's translation from Greek). The word *transformed* comes from the Greek word *metamorph*. From it, we derive the English word *metamorphosis*.

However, the ancients understood repentance to be a total-body exercise. It involved the following:

1. Mind: "I [Jesus] have come to call . . . sinners to repentance" (Luke 5:32);
2. Mouth: "If you confess with your mouth Jesus is Lord . . ." (Rom. 10:9);
3. Heart: "and believe in your heart God raised him from the dead, you will be saved" (Rom. 10:9); and
4. Behavior: "If you love me, keep my commands" (John 14:15).

Ancient records also confirm what people in the time of Jesus understood the word to mean:

> What constitutes repentance?[5] That a sinner should abandon his sins and remove them from his thoughts, resolving in his heart, never to commit them again. . . . Similarly, he must regret the past. . . . He must verbally confess and state these matters which he resolved in his heart.[6]

---

5. Hebrew: תשובה (*teshuva*), "to return."
6. Mishneh Torah, Repentance, 2.2, with reference to these Scriptures: "Let the wicked forsake their ways" (Isa. 55:7 NIV); "After I strayed, I repented" (Jer.

Since repentance requires us to submit to God and resist the devil (James 4:7), it's an inevitable act of spiritual war.

BAPTISM—AN ACT OF SPIRITUAL WAR

Moving forward, I'll show how early Christians maintained the *same* understanding as the ancient Jews on baptism and fasting. Both actions are clearly linked to repentance and spiritual warfare.

As discussed in the previous chapter, ancient Jews considered baptism an act of cleansing oneself from the impurity of idols,[7] and, of course, the influence behind an idol is a demon (Deut. 32:17; 1 Cor. 10:20). Since baptism is a sign of repentance, they expected a change in behavior. This is why converts to Judaism were required to:

1. Submit to a background check and a test for sincerity;
2. Demonstrate understanding in the basics of the faith;
3. Renounce idolatry; and
4. Obey the seven universal "Noahide Laws":[8]
    a. do not worship idols;
    b. do not blaspheme God's Name;

31:19 NIV); and "We will never again say 'Our gods' to what our own hands have made" (Hosea 14:3 NIV).

7. BT, Sotah 12b.

8. These were commandments, believed by ancient Jews, that were handed down from Adam to Noah and binding on all humans. See Eugene Korn, ed., "Noahide Covenant: Theology and Jewish Law Text," Boston College Center for Christian-Jewish Learning, accessed April 7, 2023, https://www.bc.edu/content/dam/files/research_sites/cjl/texts/cjrelations/resources/sourcebook/Noahide_cov enant.htm.

    c. do not murder;

    d. do not commit adultery or sexual immorality;

    e. do not steal;

    f. do not eat flesh torn from a living animal or consume its blood; and

    g. establish courts to ensure justice.

Then the convert was baptized.[9]

Notice how John the Baptist employs aspects of these customs with those coming out to be baptized by him (Luke 3:7–14 NIV):

1. Test of sincerity (v. 7): "You brood of vipers! Who warned you to flee from the coming wrath?"
2. Call to obedience (v. 8): "Produce fruit in keeping with repentance."
3. Background checks:
   a. Crowd (vv. 10–11): "'What should we do then?' the crowd asked. John answered, 'Anyone who has two shirts should share with the one who has none, and anyone who has food should do the same.'"
   b. Tax collectors (vv. 12–13): "'Teacher,' they asked, 'what should we do?' [He answered], 'Don't collect any more than you are required to.'"
   c. Soldiers (v. 14): "'And what should we do?' He replied, 'Don't extort money and don't accuse people falsely—be content with your pay.'"

---

9. Mishneh Torah, Issurei Biah 14.1–7; Tosefta, Avodah Zarah 9.4; BT, Sanhedrin 56a.24, 56b.1.

Again, as even the Gospels validate, baptism is a sign of repentance—changed behavior was expected.

It's no wonder we see nearly identical procedures among early Christians. In like fashion, they taught that, before we believed in God, our hearts were full of idols and our bodies were the houses of demons.[10] Also, Christian converts were required to adhere to the same four basic requirements:

1. Submit to a background check and a test for sincerity:

> Inquiry shall likewise be made about the professions and trades of those who are brought to be admitted to the faith. If a man is a pander, he must desist or be rejected. If a man is a sculptor or painter, he must be charged not to make idols; if he does not desist he must be rejected. . . . A gladiator or a trainer of gladiators, or a huntsman [in the barbaric shows], or anyone connected with these [murderous] shows, or a public official in charge of gladiatorial exhibitions must desist or be rejected. A pagan priest or anyone who tends idols must desist or be rejected. . . . An enchanter, an astrologer, a diviner, a soothsayer, a user of magic verses . . . a [fraudster] . . . must desist or be rejected. . . . If a man has a concubine, he must desist and marry legally; if he is unwilling, he must be rejected.[11]

2. Demonstrate understanding in the basics of the faith.[12]

---

10. *Epistle of Barnabas* 16.7.
11. Hippolytus, *Apostolic Tradition* 16.9–24.
12. Hippolytus, *Apostolic Tradition* 16.1.

3. Renounce idolatry, specifically Satan and his works:

   a. Tertullian (c. AD 155–220): "When we are going to enter the water, but a little before . . . we disown the devil and his pomp and his angels."[13]

   b. Hippolytus (c. AD 170–235): "Then, the elder, taking hold of each of those about to be baptized, shall command him to renounce, saying, 'I renounce you, Satan, and all your servants and all your works.'"[14]

   c. Apostolic Constitutions (c. AD 375–380): "Let, therefore, the candidate for baptism declare thus in his renunciation: 'I renounce Satan, and his works, and his pomps, and his worships, and his angels, and his inventions, and all things that are under him.'"[15]

   d. Ambrose (c. AD 339–397): "Recall what you were asked, and remember what you answered. You renounced the devil and his works, the world with its luxury and pleasures."[16]

   e. John Chrysostom (c. AD 347–407): "Now he who repents, no longer touches the same matters of which he repented. On this account, also, we are bidden to say, 'I renounce you, Satan,' in order that we may never more return to him."[17]

13. Tertullian, *The Soldiers' Chaplet* (or *De Corona*), chap. 3, https://www.tertullian.org.

14. Hippolytus, *Apostolic Tradition* 21.9.

15. *Apostolic Constitutions* 7.41, https://www.newadvent.org/fathers/07157.htm.

16. Ambrose, *On the Mysteries* 2.5, https://www.newadvent.org/fathers/07157.htm.

17. John Chrysostom, *Instructions to Catechumens*, Second Instruction, 3.1, https://www.newadvent.org/fathers/07157.htm.

4. Obey the teachings of Christ passed down through
   the New Testament with oversight from His
   Apostles.[18]

As we discovered in the previous chapter, Christian converts were not allowed to be baptized if they were still demonized.[19] How did they determine this? It's quite possible
demons surfaced while people were renouncing the devil and
his works. This action could have aroused the evil spirits who
influenced their sinful behaviors. As one scholar points out,
the historical practice of ensuring a convert was expelled of
demons enabled "the person to make that renunciation."[20]

I recall a dramatic counseling session I held with a young
lady. I was trying to lead her through a prayer of rededica-
tion, but she kept hearing a threatening voice in her head
shouting, "Don't do it! Don't do it!"

It took nearly two hours—fighting through her wails,
tears, and fears—to coach her through just a few sentences.
A few weeks earlier, I had baptized her. However, I discovered
that day—after the fact—that she came from a lineage of
witches. Needless to say, my pastoral care could have been
more effective for her if I had been familiar with historical
church practice.

Repentance, directly or indirectly, commences a spiritual
battle. That spiritual battle can

1. begin immediately or be delayed as the enemy awaits
   the best way to respond;

18. Matt. 28:19–20; Acts 2:42; Eph. 2:20; 3:5; 2 Pet. 3:2; Jude 17.
19. Hippolytus, *Apostolic Tradition* 20.3–4.
20. Linards Jansons, "Baptismal Exorcism: An Exercise in Liturgical Theology," *Lutheran Theological Journal* 45, no. 3 (December 2011): 185.

2. be from outside or inside the believer depending on the type of attack—temptation, harassment, or demonization;

3. range from minor to major—from implanted thoughts of doubt ("you'll be back") to full-blown outbursts ("we're not leaving"); and

4. last for a moment or a period of time.

Someone may initially argue with my conclusion by responding that all a believer has to do is submit to God, resist the devil, and he will flee (James 4:7). But please read that verse again. The believer's response still requires them to resist the devil, thus making my point.

FASTING—AN ACT OF SPIRITUAL WAR TOO

Like baptism, fasting is also an act of spiritual war due to its historical link to repentance. In the Bible, people fasted for multiple reasons, including:

1. To show dependence on God for guidance or protection (Ezra 8:21–23; Acts 13:2–3);

2. To strengthen devotion to God (Matt. 17:20–21; Luke 2:36–37);

3. To validate the sincerity of their prayers (Ezra 8:23; Ps. 35:13);

4. To express sorrow due to a public calamity (Neh. 1:4; Esther 4:3; Dan. 9:2–3); and

5. To humble themselves before God as a sign of repentance (Isa. 58:3–7; Jon. 3:7–10; 4:11).

145

The phrase "afflict yourselves" became a biblical way of referring to fasting (Lev. 16:31; 23:27, 32; Num. 29:7). Also, its link to repentance is conclusive. Actually, fasting could be understood as either expressing repentance or reinforcing it. An ancient rabbi rhetorically asked, "If you fast because of your sins, and then go out and commit the same sins over again, what have you gained by going without food?"[21] Likewise, a modern pastor advised on social media, "If you're fasting and cussing or fasting and fornicating or fasting and lying, you need to eat!"

The views on fasting remain the same for Old and New Covenant believers. Notice how James borrows Old Testament imagery of weeping and mourning, then blends fasting and baptismal concepts with repentance:

1. "Return to me [the Lord] with all your heart, with fasting, with weeping, and with mourning" (Joel 2:12).
2. "Wash your hands . . . purify your hearts . . . afflict[22] yourselves, mourn, and weep . . . humble yourself before the Lord, and He will exalt you" (James 4:8–10, author's translation from Greek).

JESUS FASTED FOR THE SAME REASON MOSES DID

So why did Jesus fast? For the answer, we first must determine why Moses fasted. Speaking to the Israelites, he declares:

---

21. Ben Sirach (Ecclesiasticus) 34:26.
22. Greek: ταλαιπωρέω (talaipōreō), "to be afflicted; to feel afflicted and miserable" (Thayer, 5196).

I threw myself down before the LORD for forty days and nights. I ate no bread and drank no water because of the great sin you had committed by doing what the LORD hated, provoking him to anger. I feared that the furious anger of the LORD, which turned him against you, would drive him to destroy you. But again he listened to me. (Deut. 9:18–19 NLT)

Moses reminds them of the time he returned from Mount Sinai to find them worshiping an idol. God threatened to destroy them, but Moses interceded (Exod. 32:10–20). Therefore, this is an example of intercessory fasting—intervening with God for the guilt of another.

Intercessory fasting is confirmed when we look at how the Bible compares Moses and Jesus:

Moses	Jesus
Moses survived Pharaoh's massacre of male babies (Exod. 1:15–16; 2:2–10).	*Jesus* survived Herod's massacre of male babies (Matt. 2:13–14, 16).
Moses departed Egypt (Exod. 12:40–41).	*Jesus* departed Egypt (Matt. 2:15, 19–21).
Moses was "baptized" (Exod. 14:22).[23]	*Jesus* was baptized (Matt. 3:13–17).
Moses fasted forty days on behalf of the Israelites (Deut. 9:10–20).	*Jesus* fasted forty days on behalf of the Israelites (Matt. 4:2).
Moses was spiritually tested (Deut. 8:2).	*Jesus* was spiritually tested (Matt. 4:1).

Moses predicted, "The LORD your God will raise up for you a prophet like me from among you, from your fellow Israelites. You must listen to him" (Deut. 18:15 NIV). Although the original thought may have applied to godly prophets throughout Israel's history, the singular use of the word led Jews to expect

23. Notice the Apostle Paul refers to this historical event as a metaphorical baptism: "They were all baptized into Moses in the cloud and in the sea" (1 Cor. 10:2 NIV).

one prophet, specifically the Savior.[24] This is why the Apostle Peter applies it to Jesus as its fulfillment (Acts 3:19–26).

The purpose in all this is to show that Jesus, although sinless (Heb. 4:15), fasted with Israel's repentance in mind. Like Moses, He pleaded with God the Father to show them mercy. As the Prophet Isaiah proclaims, Christ "made intercession for the transgressors" (Isa. 53:12 NIV).

Although Jesus fasted to intercede for Israel, the devil still deemed it an act of spiritual war. This is why he visited Jesus, and his first attempt was to convince Jesus to stop fasting (Matt. 4:1–4). Also, the devil coincidentally quoted from Psalm 91, a prayer historically used in the ancient ministry of expelling demons (vv. 5–6).[25]

To recap, fasting is an expression of repentance or a pleading with God to have mercy on those needing to repent. Since repentance involves rejecting Satan and his works, demons won't give up without a fight. The spiritual battle could be as small as being tempted one hour into your one-day fast to turn two slices of bread into a sandwich.

Considering the historical background and Scriptures above, it appears Jesus left us a few spiritual warfare examples. As the Scripture commands, "Be imitators of God, as beloved children" (Eph. 5:1).

Jesus	Us
He was led by the Holy Spirit (Matt. 4:1).	*We* need the Holy Spirit to fill us and lead us into all truth (John 16:13; Eph. 5:18).

24. I. Howard Marshall, *The Acts of the Apostles* (1915; repr., Grand Rapids: Eerdmans, 1991), 94–95.

25. Bohak, "Jewish Exorcisms Before and After the Destruction of the Second Temple," 290.

Jesus	Us
He was baptized but sinless (Matt. 3:13).	*We* are baptized as a pledge to turn away from sinful living (Acts 2:38; 1 Pet. 3:21).[26]
He fasted but didn't need to (Matt. 4:2).	*We* fast mainly to demonstrate repentance from our sins (Acts 9:1–9; James 4:9–10).
He resisted the devil's temptations with Scripture, but it was unnecessary, because He is the Word (John 1:1, 14).	*We* resist the devil by wearing the armor of God and fighting back with the dagger[27] of God's Word (Eph. 6:11–17).
He expelled the devil from His presence, but He could have commanded His angels to banish him (Matt. 4:11; 26:53).	*We* must submit to God and resist the devil, and he will flee—sometimes by command, as Jesus demonstrated (James 4:7).[28]

Likewise, to lessen casualties in this spiritual war, we must fast on behalf of others with the plea that "God may perhaps grant them repentance leading to a knowledge of the truth" (2 Tim. 2:25).

REPENTANCE—A WAY TO FIND FREEDOM FROM DEMONIZATION

Since repentance involves resisting the devil, a spiritual battle is inevitable—even if it is delayed or minor or simply centers around the temptation to give up. However, if the person proves to be demonized and the related spiritual warfare becomes more than they can bear alone, then help from experienced

26. For seasoned believers, the early church continually reminds us to live up to our baptisms. See the writings of 2 Clement 6:9 and Ignatius, *To Polycarp* 6:2.

27. Greek: μάχαιρα (*machaira*), "small sword or dagger." It is a weapon for close combat; also a large knife for killing and cutting up (Friberg, 17892).

28. In chap. 6, point 9, I show that James likely based this scriptural truth on Jesus's temptations.

believers or church leaders is strongly recommended. There are two main methods utilized today:

A. Confrontational Method—generally, in the Name of Christ Jesus:[29]

    1. Demon is discerned or commanded to reveal itself;

    2. Demon is bound in Jesus's Name;

    3. Demon is interrogated for information (name, reason, other demons present, etc.);

    4. Demonic connections are broken by confessing and renouncing associated sins; and

    5. Demon is expelled.

B. Truth Encounter Method—generally, in the Name of Christ Jesus:[30]

---

29. As an example, Dr. C. Fred Dickason summarizes the Confrontational Method:

> There must be the confident and authoritative confrontation of wicked spirits, calling for their confession that Christ is victor and that the Christian is positionally victor in Christ. The demon must be made to confess that he will obey the Lord Jesus and the counselee and leave when Jesus and the counselee agree. Then there must be a command for him to leave. If he does not leave immediately, the counselor must seek from the Christian or from the demon what ground (moral occasion) there might be for his staying in the person. That must be biblically judged and confessed and claimed back from the demon. Again he must be told in the name of Jesus to go to where Jesus sends him with all his host. This must be continued until the leading demon of all is gone, there is no more demonic response to inquiry or command, and the major demonic symptoms vanish from the Christian's experience. This is the approach in brief that has worked in many cases. Not all cases are the same, but the general principles pertain to all. (Dickason, *Demon Possession & the Christian*, 335)

30. As an example, Dr. Neil T. Anderson defines the Truth Encounter Method:

> After hearing an inquirer's story, I always ask if he or she would like to resolve their issues. No one has ever said no. Then I say, "With your permission, I will lead you through The Steps to Freedom in Christ. What is going to happen here today is not based on what I do, but what

1. Believer prays against demons surfacing or interfering with the session;

2. Believer or assistant maintains control of the session by utilizing Jesus's Name;

3. Believer, along with spiritual discernment, inventories areas of sin in their life;

4. Believer counters Satan's deceptions with God's truth; and

5. Believer experiences freedom by confessing and renouncing identified sins.

The true stories in this book involve elements from both methods as various circumstances dictated. Admittedly, the Confrontational Method is the example we witness in the New Testament and early church history and is still employed today. Yet the Truth Encounter Method is very effective. A resource I continue to use after 30 years of ministry is a workbook entitled *Steps to Freedom in Christ*.[31] It contains checklists of specific sins because a believer may not be aware

---

you do." . . . It is important to pay close attention to the inquirer. If you see her eyes starting to cloud over or look around the room, get her attention immediately. Even in the most difficult cases you don't have to lose control. Some people have been conditioned to have a thought and then carry it out. It may seem to them that they have no control, but in reality, they do. Some have told me that they never even considered the possibility that they didn't have to obey the thought. . . . In extreme cases, some inquirers could go catatonic. If that happens, say out loud, "Satan, you have no authority here. You can open your eyes now," and the inquirer will. . . . Others will feel nauseous, and when they share that, I say, "Thank you for sharing that. The nauseous feeling will be gone when we are done." That has been true in every case I've handled. (Neil T. Anderson, *Bondage Breaker*, rev. and exp. ed. [Eugene, OR: Harvest House, 2019], 201–2)

31. Neil T. Anderson, *Steps to Freedom in Christ* (Bloomington, MN: Bethany House, 2017).

of actions from which they must repent. (With permission, I share its effective spiritual warfare prayers in the appendix.)

A believer may prefer one method over the other but incorporate elements from both. For example, Dr. C. Fred Dickason utilizes the Confrontational Method but still states, "Practically, this involves renouncing before God the devil and all his works. Any involvements in things occult and demonic must be confessed and a stand taken against them. Specific confession and renunciation are tools that strip the enemy of his assumed rights that may have allowed his influence or invasion. We have seen the enemy wince and retreat under such treatment."[32]

Dr. Neil T. Anderson utilizes the Truth Encounter Method. However, he also shares an adrenaline-inducing story of when he confronted an evil spirit while counseling a severely demonized woman: "During the session, the woman—who was big and husky—suddenly rose from her chair and walked toward me with a menacing look. At that point I was glad that the weapons of our warfare are not of the flesh, because I would have had a difficult time defending myself against a demonized person her size. Instead, I spoke these words based on 1 John 5:18—not to the woman, because she was blanked out at the time, but to the evil spirit controlling her: 'I'm a child of God, and the evil one can't touch me. Sit down right now.' She stopped in her tracks and returned to her chair."[33]

Yet a third method was introduced in the 1590s by a pastor named John Darrell. He was famous for helping people find

---

32. Dickason, *Demon Possession & the Christian*, 249–50.
33. Anderson, *Bondage Breaker*, rev. and exp. ed., 90.

freedom from demonization through prayer and fasting.[34] This approach seems practical, if it includes all the elements of repentance as previously discussed.

No matter what method you use, if the related spiritual warfare becomes more than the client or assisting believers can bear, help from more experienced believers is highly recommended. Also remember, as a rule, repentance is the root to finding and maintaining freedom in Christ. As Jesus warned, there's a dangerous link between unrepentance and a worse state of demonization (Matt. 12:43–45).

Very early in my career I was asked to cast a demon out of a young lady who demonstrated clear supernatural signs of being inhabited. I arrived at the home with another minister. Neither of us knew what we were doing, because we were ordained in a denomination that neither taught nor trained on the subject. However, I recently had completed a systematic theology class in which we studied angels and demons, so the other minister deferred to me on this matter.

When the moment came for me to cast out the demon, the other minister nodded for me to proceed behind the lady, who was seated in a particular place in the living room. As I was about to lay my hands on the woman's head, I had an immediate vision of her lifting me over her head and slamming me onto the coffee table in the center of the room. Startled, I instantly returned to my seat and abruptly ended the session. Shortly after I sat down, the woman said, "The demon told me, 'If he touches you, lift him up and slam him onto the table.'" Well, it was clear I needed some training![35]

---

34. Caciola, "Exorcism," 2931.
35. In chap. 6 (point 4), I verify there is no biblical example of Jesus or his disciples laying hands on those who were demonized. Also, I show from church

Sadly, I don't know if she ever found freedom from that demon. However, what I do know is that in subsequent conversations with her, she admitted to having unconfessed sin in her life. Every time we discussed repentance, she refused. I rarely have a problem convincing people to confess their sins, but leading them to renounce the sins is typically a challenge. This is why the Bible declares, "The one who confesses and renounces [their sins] finds mercy" (Prov. 28:13b NIV).

Jesus's ministry of expelling demons is one of the proofs the kingdom of God is in operation, and He wants all people to enjoy the liberties that come with allegiance to Him. This is why He continues to empower the subjects of His kingdom to expel demons. Our loving God and King pleads with us, "Repent and live!" (Ezek. 18:32; 2 Pet. 3:9).

An ancient rabbi advised his students, "Repent one day before your death."[36] The students astutely asked, "Does anyone know on what day he will die?" He retorted, "This is all the more reason it's good advice! One should repent today in case he dies tomorrow. By following this advice, one will spend every day of his life repenting."[37]

Remember, godly sorrow leads to a life of repentance—it breaks the chain and frees us by declaring, "Never again!" (2 Cor. 7:10).

---

history the practice of doing so was an evolution when the bishops (around the third century) brought the ministry of exorcism under the oversight of those with the gift of healing. Of course, healing indeed involves the laying on of hands; thus, the practice. However, I'm sure those who practice laying hands on those who are demonized use discernment and/or cease to do so when the client's response is violent.

36. Pirkei Avot 2.10.
37. Shabbat 153a.5, with my paraphrase.

PART 3

PASTORAL EXPERIENCES

24 TRUE STORIES

9

IT WASN'T DEPRESSION

This chapter kicks off the section where I discuss an additional 24 true stories about specific demonic intrusions (chapters 9–17). In the previous chapters, I shared my personal encounters (chapters 1–3), then we analyzed biblical insights (chapters 4–8). Now I believe we're prepared to understand these pastoral cases—the first relating to depression.

Scripture commands us, "Always be joyful" (1 Thess. 5:16 NLT), but what if you're always sad? Victoria grew up in humble circumstances. She also experienced unspoken woundedness as a child. Escaping her community for a better life, she went off to college and graduated before joining the military. It was in this professional setting that I met her.

Victoria was smart and talkative and enjoyed a good laugh. Yet she assured me this wasn't always the case. A few years earlier, she was a young leader eager to make a difference, but the rain cloud of sadness followed her everywhere.

She told me, "I gave my life to Christ, but my sadness didn't go away!"

One day, Victoria was in church. She looked around, witnessing all the people with their hands raised and joyfully singing, and she determined that day she was going to force herself to sing. When she did, a choking sensation overtook her. She stopped, tried again, and the choking sensation returned.

With tears in her eyes, she cried, "God, why can't I sing?" All of a sudden, she had a vision of a large snake with the face of a frog—it was sad and wounded. Sensing it was an evil spirit, she panicked and rebuked it.

A few days later, she attended her small group Bible study and shared what had happened to her, exclaiming, "It did not leave!" Fortunately, there was a mature Christian lady experienced in spiritual matters like these. She directed the small group to encircle Victoria. As she led them in prayer, Victoria immediately felt something leave her body. At that moment, joy abounded in her heart like never before. She beamed like a ray of sunshine, and everybody noticed—her small group members, coworkers, and supervisor.

During church that Sunday, she sang her heart out. After church, people approached her, marveling at her glow. Her pastor even asked, "What happened to you?" When she explained her story, he frowned and dismissed it, saying, "Christians can't have a demon."

For the first time in several days, Victoria was deflated, because if what her pastor said was true, how could she be assured she was really a Christian? The good news is Victoria was reassured by her small group of her initial profession of faith. They all understood what happened to her to be real. However, the biggest takeaway from our conversation was when she disclosed, "That 'creature' was so entrenched in my life that I couldn't tell it apart from my own feelings."

OTHER CONTRIBUTORS TO DEPRESSION

Victoria's case is an example of why we should never rule out a spiritual cause for mental health matters. However, we shouldn't automatically jump to that conclusion either. When people seek me for counseling regarding depression, I first explore the typical big rocks. Is there (1) a history of mental health treatment; (2) a recent crisis or trauma; or (3) a setback in a key relationship? When Sam sought my help for his suicidal thoughts, he replied no to all three questions. He was mystified because he'd never experienced feelings of self-harm before.

I asked if there were any recent changes to his normal routine. He stated he started working the day shift two weeks ago. Then I discovered he worked in an underground military facility. The light bulb went on—he had a vitamin D deficiency. We treated it, and Sam's suicidal ideation immediately vanished.

Another case I had involved a newlywed couple, Collin and Jessica. Six months into their marriage, they were having problems adjusting to a new region, new jobs, and a new way of life. Collin became a danger to himself. He developed a new habit—drowning his sorrows in alcohol. Echoing the concerns of Jessica, I remember clearly warning him that depression and depressants like alcohol can be a deadly combination.

At the end of our session, my pastoral intuition led me to set up an appointment to meet with him alone. We met the following week, but Collin was spiraling deeper into sadness. After the second session ended, he left my office and entered the weekend. I strongly sensed the need to pray, "Lord, please save Collin from himself."

I received a phone call from him on Monday requesting an immediate session. He arrived and told me this shocking story: "When I left your office, I was hopeless. Nothing was working out my way. Jessica and I got into an argument, so she left to stay at a friend's house. I went to the liquor store and bought a bottle of brandy. After nearly downing the whole bottle, I went into the kitchen, grabbed the sharpest knife in the drawer, laid in the bathtub, sawed both of my wrists, and waited to die. The next morning, I woke up in the bathtub, noticed the knife by my leg, then looked at the marks on my wrists. I scurried out of the tub and shouted, 'What have I just done!'"

I saw the red marks on Collin's wrists, but miraculously, the knife blade never broke the skin.

SUICIDAL VOICES AND NIGHTMARES

The military isn't exempt from the societal tragedy of suicide. All military members must complete annual suicide intervention training. Also, the military investigates every completed suicide to determine better ways to prevent them. Chaplains serve on those investigative boards along with other helping agencies. Many times clients suffering from suicidal ideation claim to hear a voice telling them, "Kill yourself." I started regularly asking my colleagues on the panels who are psychologists and psychiatrists:

1. "How can a chemical imbalance produce a personal voice?"

2. "How can our neurotransmitters randomly create thoughts we are opposed to thinking?"[1]

Hoping for a different answer each time, I always received the same one: "We don't know." Ironically, scientists now admit there's zero evidence depression is caused by a chemical imbalance in the brain. Molecular biologist Dr. Laura Sanders confesses, "The hard truth is that despite decades of sophisticated research, we still don't understand what depression is. There are no clear descriptions of it, and no obvious signs of it in the brain or blood."[2] Again, this is why we should never rule out a spiritual cause for mental health matters.

In one such case, I met with a young man named Carter. He hadn't attended church in a while and was not in a good place spiritually. However, he requested to see me, not necessarily because he was ready to rededicate his life to Christ. Instead, he had started hearing voices throughout the day telling him, "You need to kill yourself." Then he started having nightmares in which he saw himself in a pool of his own blood. Before this, Carter never had suicidal thoughts or considered suicide an option. He claimed, "They just came out of nowhere."

I invited him to journey through the *Steps to Freedom in Christ*. After the session, the voices stopped. I contacted Carter several years later, and he stated the suicidal voices and nightmares never returned.

1. I credit Dr. Neil Anderson, whose research prompted me to ask those questions. See his book *The Bondage Breaker—The Next Step* (Eugene, OR: Harvest House, 2011), 14–15.
2. Laura Sanders, "A Chemical Imbalance Doesn't Explain Depression. So What Does?," *Science News*, February 24, 2023, https://www.sciencenews.org/article/chemical-imbalance-explain-depression.

THERE WAS A "SOURCE" TO HIS SADNESS TOO

While I typically recommend mental health therapy for depression and suicidal ideation, I also consider that the source could be spiritual. Bruce is an example of this. No matter how hard he tried, Bruce frequently failed to achieve objectives. Growing up in a big family, feeling overlooked, and not measuring up to the accomplishments of other family members left him unsure of himself. When he came to my office, he was soaked in sadness from his camouflage cap all the way to the soles of his boots. It felt like we were wading through water in our counseling sessions. Whenever I felt we made progress, the riptides of hopelessness pulled him back into the sea of despair. I convinced him to use some of his vacation days and attend a Freedom in Christ Conference.[3] Later he emailed me:

> I kept hearing doubts in my head, "This conference won't help. What a waste of time." When the conference started, my doubts proved right, but I stayed. Halfway through, something happened. I felt something like a heavy coat lift off of me when I renounced bitterness from my childhood. I can't remember ever being this happy before. Thank you for not giving up on me.

Jesus declared, "Blessed are those who mourn, for they shall be comforted" (Matt. 5:4). In this life, everyone will taste the bitter tears of sadness. Yet joy is a fruit of being indwelled by the Holy Spirit (Gal. 5:22–23)—and the more we yield to Him, the more we also taste of that wonderful fruit.

3. If interested, visit https://www.ficm.org for details.

There are helpful prayers on anxiety and on suicidal tendencies located in the appendix of this book. Along with a holistic approach including mental, physical, and social remedies, I recommend believers fast and pray—especially if the other efforts yield no relief. And if the source proves to be of demonic origin, rely on the authority of Christ to successfully confront it.

10

IT CAME THROUGH THE MUSIC AND THE MOVIE

The military chaplaincy afforded me the opportunity to preach the Gospel on nearly every continent in the world. I met some amazing and extraordinary people on my journeys. Jonathan was one of them. He was a uniquely talented musician, highly skilled on multiple instruments. I was thrilled to have him serve in one of my church bands because his talents highly elevated the quality of our music.

Eventually, I developed a pastoral concern. Every Sunday during praise and worship, Jonathan was lively and energetic. Then during the sermon, he would doze like a bear in hibernation. Before you blame it on the speaker (i.e., me), you should know that no one else was dozing. At the conclusion of the church service, he instantly awoke like he was oversaturated on energy drinks, then started leading a jam session on stage. This happened for three weeks straight.

By this time, I had several years of experience in spiritual warfare. I learned not to ignore a pastoral suspicion. So one day I asked Jonathan if we could meet. He walked into the office smiling and full of zest. After some pleasantries, I shared my observation—especially the part about him having a noticeable snore the previous Sunday. He had no idea he was dozing off during the sermon.

I inquired if he got enough sleep at night, and he assured me he got a full night's rest. I asked him if he slept well the night before. He assured me he did. Then I asked him if we could do a short experiment—to read him a few verses of Scripture. He agreed. I opened up to one of my favorite passages, Romans 12:1–2 (NASB). I began to read, "I urge you, therefo—" Jonathan's chin hit his chest, and he was in a full doze.

My personal practice is not to touch anyone I believe to be demonized, so I called his name: "Jonathan, Jonathan, JONATHAN!" He woke up confused.

When I told him I was unable to complete the first verse before he dozed, he laughed. "Are you kidding me? That really happened?" He asked if we could repeat it. I recommended bringing in a trusted friend. He agreed, so I walked out of my office and invited one of the band members who was in the sanctuary praying to join us. After the three of us sat down, I opened my Bible and read, "I urge you, therefo—" and Jonathan dozed off again.

Jonathan and I explored the possible causes of this. He also realized he had an aversion to Bible studies, so we prayerfully traced this back as far as he could remember. We found the root: it was around the time he joined a secular band. Before that, he attended Sunday school—even a small group Bible study. Shortly after joining this band, he totally lost interest in reading or studying Scripture. How could this be?

WE MUST MONITOR THE CONTENT OF SONGS

The earliest historical and lexical conclusions[1] of Ezekiel 28:13 teach that Satan's original body was embedded with the musical instruments of tambourines[2] and flutes.[3] This indicates Satan, before his fall, played a musical role in heavenly worship. This could be a reason he takes a special interest in the music industry. He knows music can be a powerful means of invoking the supernatural:

1. God is enthroned on the praises of His people (Ps. 22:3);

2. Worship music can subdue demons (1 Sam. 16:14–23); and

3. Worship songs can ignite the gift of prophecy (2 Kings 3:15; 1 Chron. 25:1).

We all know how God can bless us through a song, lifting us out of the mire of despair and propelling us upward in hope. Music—especially with an intentional message—can

---

1. The Hebrew of the latter part of Ezekiel 28:13 (מלאכת תפיך ונקביך) describes Satan's created body as also consisting of "the workmanship of your timbrels and pipes." This rendering has historical precedence as validated by the renowned German scholar Franz Eugen Schlachter, who understood the Hebrew phrase as referring to musical instruments (tambourines and flutes) in his German translation of the Bible, Schlachter 2000. Also, this is verified by lexical support in my footnotes below.

2. Hebrew: תף (tōph); in plural construct, "timbrel, tambourine—sign of merriment, gladness" (BDB, 10623).

3. Hebrew: נקב (neqeb); in plural construct, the verb means to "pierce or bore a hole," and the noun reflects a term used of a technician (i.e., work of a jeweler) who pierces or bores holes (BDB, 6297). Since the KJV, NKJV, and YLT translate it as "pipe," it could be understood as a flute (a rod bored with holes). This pairs perfectly with the "timbrels" for the purpose of music.

be orchestrated to draw us nearer to God or closer to His archenemy.

Dr. Alexander Pantelyat, a neurologist and codirector of the Johns Hopkins Center for Music and Medicine, declares, "Just listening to music activates more brain regions simultaneously than any other human activity."[4] Research also reveals relaxing music can lower stress, heart rate, and blood pressure. Additionally, it can enhance memory and motor skills and simultaneously connect both halves of the brain.[5]

Dr. Craig A. Anderson, distinguished professor of liberal arts and sciences in the department of psychology at Iowa State University, warns that violent songs create aggressive thoughts and feelings with negative consequences for the real world. His major conclusion from his research is this: "Content matters."[6]

Typically, soft music is relaxing, upbeat music stirs energy, and love songs foster romance. However, we can underestimate the spiritual impact of songs that contradict the teachings of Christ. Consider these commands:

1. "Keep your mouth free of perversity; keep corrupt talk far from your lips" (Prov. 4:24 NIV).

2. "Do not let any unwholesome talk come out of your mouths, but only what is helpful for building others up according to their needs, that it may benefit those who listen" (Eph. 4:29 NIV).

---

4. Alexander Pantelyat, quoted in Marc Shapiro, "Harnessing the Healing Power of Music," *Dome*, Johns Hopkins Medicine, August 31, 2022, https://www.hopkins medicine.org/news/articles/2022/08/harnessing-the-healing-power-of-music.

5. Shapiro, "Harnessing the Healing Power of Music."

6. Craig Anderson, "Violent Music Lyrics Increase Aggressive Thoughts and Feelings," American Psychological Association, 2003, https://www.apa.org/news/press/releases/2003/05/violent-songs.

Thus, God especially prohibits lyrics that promote these Second Death Sins:

Consolidated List of Second Death Sins (1 Cor. 6:9–10; Gal. 5:19–21; Rev. 21:8)			
1. sexual immorality	8. verbal abuse[8]	15. fits of rage	22. unbelief[17]
2. idolatry	9. impurity	16. selfish ambition	23. vileness
3. adultery	10. debauchery[9]	17. dissensions[13]	24. murder
4. homosexuality[7]	11. witchcraft[10]	18. factions[14]	25. sorcery
5. stealing	12. hatred	19. envy[15]	26. lying
6. greed	13. discord[11]	20. orgies	27. *and the like*
7. drunkenness	14. jealousy[12]	21. cowardness[16]	

"Do not be deceived. . . . I warn you . . . those who live like this will not inherit the kingdom of God" (1 Cor. 6:9; Gal. 5:21 NIV).

7. This one word is actually two words in Greek: (1) μαλακός (*malakos*), the effeminate participant in same-sex intercourse (DANK, 4071); and (2) ἀρσενοκοίτης (*arsenokoitēs*), the dominant participant in same-sex intercourse (DANK, 931).

8. Greek: λοίδορος (*loidoros*), one who abuses another with speech (Friberg, 17453).

9. Greek: ἀσέλγεια (*aselgeia*), sensuality (Friberg, 3805).

10. Greek: φαρμακεία (*pharmakeia*); from it we derive "pharmacy," involving, in a forbidden way, "the use or the administering of drugs" usually for sorcery (Thayer, 5532).

11. Greek: ἔρις (*eris*), one who starts fights (Friberg, 11452).

12. Greek: ζῆλος (*zēlos*) can mean "zeal," but "in a negative sense, it is passion for one's self-interests in the face of what appears to be competition" (DANK, 2912); thus, we can act maliciously against another for fear of them taking away something belonging to us.

13. Greek: διχοστασία (*dichostasia*), one who starts disagreements that threaten unity (DANK, 1719).

14. Greek: αἵρεσις (*hairesis*), one who separates communities usually through false teaching (Friberg, 668).

15. Greek: φθόνος (*phthonos*), "in a negative sense *envy, jealousy* over the good success of another" (Friberg, 28003); leads one to seize from or sabotage another (i.e., Cain murdered his brother Abel due to envy [Gen. 4:7–8; Heb. 11:4]).

16. Greek: δειλός (*deilos*), "Christians who give up their faith out of fear of people" (Thayer, 1225).

17. Greek: ἄπιστος (*apistos*), no faith (DANK, 722); in this case, it refers to those who reject faith in Christ Jesus.

Also, the Bible commands us, "Whatever you do, whether in word or deed, do it all in the name of the Lord Jesus, giving thanks to God the Father through him" (Col. 3:17 NIV). How do songs meet this requirement? As a test, if you're not comfortable saying "in Jesus's Name, amen" after a song, then it's probably forbidden.

Have you ever noticed a song can replay in your mind long after you've turned off the music? Neurologists and psychologists inform us that music—like no other medium—affects the brain and influences behavior. Since that's the case, what do you do if you're in an environment where music with ungodly content is played and you have no choice in the matter? I discovered playing Christian music can override it. Nevertheless, given the scientifically and spiritually proven effects music with bad content can have on us, I recommend you make reasonable efforts to avoid it altogether.

The mind is our battlefield (2 Cor. 10:5). If music can move the masses in a direction Satan desires, it's no surprise he offers fame and fortune to artists who will bow the knee to him (Matt. 4:9). Even Theophilus, the Bishop of Antioch (c. AD 180), warned of specific types of demons expelled from people in his day: "The deceiving spirits confess[ed] themselves [to be] the demons who once worked in the poets."[18]

Jonathan, the young musician who would doze during sermons, discovered that many of the songs he rehearsed and played in his secular band promoted content from Second Death Sins. This antibiblical content was so strong that it overrode his ability to concentrate on the Bible. He confessed

18. Theophilus, *Ad Autolycum* 2.8.

the sin of ignorance, renounced Satan and all his works, and refused to ever play or listen to those songs again. From that day forward, Jonathan was fully awake at church every Sunday.

IT PROTECTED ITS MUSIC

One year, my ministerial team and I led a conference on the dangers of music with unwholesome messages. We were able to show undeniable research validating clear demonic ties to certain lyrics and satanic imagery associated with some album covers, dance routines, and award show trophies.

There was a young lady who couldn't make it to the conference, so she requested the recording. After her work shift, she watched the presentation and was petrified by the research—especially since her husband owned albums from many of the musical artists. She went to bed that night determined to speak with her husband in the morning. Before she could talk with him, she called the church in full panic: "I watched the DVD you lent me. Shortly after I went to bed, a shadow creature started choking me. As I gasped for air, I begged it to release me, and it told me, 'I'll only release you if you promise not to tell your husband what you learned about the music.' I agreed to the promise, and it released me."

There was nothing we could do to calm her down. She refused to even come by the church to drop off the DVD. One of the associate ministers had to meet her at a location of her choosing to retrieve it from her. As far as we know, she never told her husband and kept her promise to that shadow creature.

IT CAME THROUGH THE MOVIE TOO

When I was young, I loved the thrill of watching a good horror movie. However, shortly after I submitted to the Lordship of Jesus Christ, it instantly felt like I was in one. With the dark encounters I share in this book, hopefully you realize why I highly discourage horror movies: "For God has not given us a spirit of fear, but of power and of love and of a sound mind" (2 Tim. 1:7 NKJV). If demons ever surface and you strive to confront them, they will try to use fear tactics to intimidate you.

So I started watching sci-fi movies instead. However, just like I share above about music, I discovered you still need to monitor the content.

One day, I was all alone at home watching a Bigfoot movie. Eventually, a scene appeared in which the people gathered for a séance. As they were chanting, suddenly the lights in my home began to flicker. Having extensive experience with house cleansings due to paranormal activities, I suspected what I was up against. So I turned off the TV, grabbed my Bible, and went out to my back porch to prepare myself to pray over my home.

As I was reading my Bible, I heard the dead bolt click into a locked position. Immediately, I looked back, and there was no one there. Then I opened the location feature on my smartphone, and it confirmed all my family members were away from home. Now I was certain of what I was up against. For the record, this back door had an alignment problem requiring us to lift the doorknob and push the door fully closed before we could twist the dead bolt into its socket. So it was not possible for it to slip and lock itself.

The front door was already locked, and I had no key on me, so I sat on my back porch and waited for about 30 minutes until my wife arrived home. Afterward, I used the house-cleansing prayer found in the appendix of this book to expel my home of evil spirits, and I had no more paranormal issues.

During the height of the coronavirus, churches were forced to stream worship services online due to limits on gathering sizes. Nevertheless, many of us discovered we could have a meaningful spiritual experience through our televisions. Satan tries to deceptively emulate God through the same avenues. This is why, in relation to all media, we must guard our eyes, our ears, and our hearts (Prov. 4:23; Eccles. 7:5; Matt. 18:9).

Remember, Jesus refers to us as the salt and light of the world (Matt. 5:13–14). Salt preserves what's good, and light exposes what's bad. Therefore, it's our responsibility to influence culture, not be influenced by it (Rom. 12:2; Eph. 2:1–2).

For the record, demons couldn't care less whether or not you're aware your media is providing an opening to them. Their goal is to infiltrate your life by any means necessary—they don't even consider your children off-limits. So close and lock all your "windows" and "doors," because Jesus warns the "thief" will come to steal, kill, and destroy (John 10:10).

11

STARTLED BY TAROT CARDS, CRYSTALS, AND OUIJA BOARDS

I was in the middle of leading a small group Bible study when Michelle quietly entered the room and found a seat. To me, the best Bible studies are like an interactive sport. I toss a scriptural question into the middle of the ring, then let the students wrestle for the right answer. According to Michelle, that night's study was mind-blowing!

A few weeks later, Michelle knocked on my office door, and I invited her to take a seat. She paused, took a deep breath, then began: "My friend dragged me to one of your Bible studies last month. When I heard your teaching on sorcery and witchcraft, I was deeply troubled. Afterward, my friend joined me as I destroyed my tarot cards and crystals. The next day, I noticed I had no need for my medicine, because the stomach ailment I had for ten years suddenly disappeared. I stopped taking my medicine and waited to see if my pain would return. It has been several weeks now, and I've had no stomach problems!"

Michelle told me even more: "When I was sixteen, I developed a mysterious stomach illness. My mom took me to the doctor, but it was one failed treatment after another. They prescribed medicine, but it didn't help. I underwent a stomach scope, but it revealed nothing abnormal. The illness became so terrible I was even hospitalized. The doctors convinced my parents I needed my gallbladder removed, but that surgery didn't improve my condition. This went on for years. But the day after I destroyed my tarot cards and crystals, I woke up, and for the first time in 10 years, I had no stomach pain! I waited all this time to tell you to ensure it wasn't a fluke."

After a moment of rejoicing, I asked Michelle, "Just out of curiosity, when did you start utilizing tarot cards and crystals?" She thought for a moment, cupped her mouth, then gasped. "When I was sixteen!"

I had the privilege of baptizing her a few weeks later. Coincidentally, our paths crossed 14 years later at a leadership event. By then she was a senior executive, but that didn't stop her from letting out a loud "Oh my goodness" and hugging me like a long-lost friend. It was a decade and a half later, and the stomach pain had never returned—she was completely healed.

OTHER FORBIDDEN SPIRITUAL PRACTICES

The Bible clearly forbids sorcery, witchcraft, and the use of psychics and mediums:

> Let no one be found among you who sacrifices their son
> or daughter in the fire, who practices divination or sorcery,

174

interprets omens, engages in witchcraft, or casts spells, or who is a medium or spiritist or who consults the dead. (Deut. 18:10–11 NIV)

Also, Scripture forbids the use of astrology and horoscopes to predict one's future:

Disaster will come upon you, and you will not know how to conjure it away. . . . Keep on, then, with your magic spells and with your many sorceries, which you have labored at since childhood. . . . All the counsel you have received has only worn you out! Let your astrologers come forward, those stargazers who make predictions month by month, let them save you from what is coming upon you. Surely they are like stubble; the fire will burn them up. They cannot even save themselves from the power of the flame. These are not coals for warmth; this is not a fire to sit by. (Isa. 47:11–14 NIV)

These practices fall into the category of Second Death Sins that prevent people from inheriting the kingdom of God (1 Cor. 6:9–10; Gal. 5:19–21; Rev. 21:8).

For clarity, there is a difference between astronomy and astrology. God allows us to use the science of astronomy to plan an annual calendar based on the consistent patterns of the sun and moon: "Let them be signs to mark the seasons, days, and years" (Gen. 1:14 NLT). However, God forbids us to use the religious practice of astrology to seek spiritual guidance about people, ourselves, or the future. As the Prophet Isaiah advises, "Should not a people inquire of their God?" (Isa. 8:19 NIV).

As Michelle's testimony confirms, God forbids astrology, sorcery, and witchcraft, because demons use these practices to lead people astray—plus infiltrate their lives. Any spiritual information that is not obtained from the Holy Spirit comes from an *unholy* spirit. This is why sorcerers who submitted to the Lordship of Jesus Christ "brought their incantation books and burned them at a public bonfire. The value of the books was several million dollars" (Acts 19:19 NLT).

OUIJA BOARDS, A HAUNTED BONFIRE, AND A T-SHIRT TAG

Michelle destroyed her tarot cards and crystals, and the Bible tells us newly converted sorcerers burned their scrolls in the fire. They did so because they discovered there was an evil presence behind these items. This is why God forbids them.

Ouija boards are another concern. It was recently reported in the news that 28 Colombian school girls were hospitalized after playing with one. Their symptoms included loss of consciousness, fainting spells, extreme anxiety, and other mysterious symptoms.[1] If it's just an innocent game, why did it cause such negative effects on the health of those young girls? I visited a well-known retail store. In the entrance, they were selling a large Halloween candy bag with a Ouija board embroidered in its fabric. Beware—Satan does not consider our children off-limits.

A few years ago, some of my colleagues went on a missionary trip to China. Upon their return, they received a package in the mail. They opened the box to discover an authentic,

1. Ben Cost, "28 Girls Hospitalized with 'Anxiety' after Playing with Ouija Board," *New York Post*, March 7, 2023, https://nypost.com/2023/03/07/28-girls-hospitalized-for-anxiety-after-ouija-board-game.

hand-carved Ouija board. Although it was a gesture of kind-ness, they realized they could not keep it, so they ignited their fire pit and tossed the Ouija board into it. They ran into the house terrified when the board began to scream and howl!

Another friend of mine grew up in a non-Christian home. He had a little brother who regularly consulted a Ouija board. So one day he decided to poke some fun with it. He was wear-ing a colorful tie-dyed shirt, so he asked the Ouija board, "What color shirt am I wearing?" He said it sat in "thinking mode" for a while, then it started spelling out "*k-a-l-e-i-d-o-s-c-o-p-e*." It was the brand name of the T-shirt located on the neck tag!

"Come out from them and be separate, says the Lord. Touch no unclean thing, and I will receive you. . . . I will be a Father to you, and you will be my sons and daughters, says the Lord Almighty" (2 Cor. 6:17–18 NIV).

177

12

SOMETHING ELSE CAME WITH THE PORN

High school sweethearts Daryl and Chelsea graduated and got married right before Daryl left for military training. Chelsea didn't grow up in a Christian home, but her grandmother took her to church whenever Chelsea visited. Daryl had never gone to church and over time became agnostic—there was something out there, but he just didn't know what it was.

Both were virgins when they married. Their union was more than they ever imagined. Although they were living a long distance away from their families, their lives were blissful, loving, and fulfilling. They were inseparable. However, midway through Daryl's first military tour, he came home one day, took off his uniform, showered, rushed through dinner, then went into the bedroom requesting privacy. Chelsea figured he'd had a stressful day, so she gave him his space. However, it happened again the next day—then the next. When he turned down sex for the third night in a row, she knew something was wrong.

LOVE TWISTED AND TAINTED

Chelsea didn't like conflict, but she finally mustered up the courage to ask him if everything was okay. At first, Daryl was dismissive, but Chelsea was persistent. Reluctantly, he admitted to watching porn on his smartphone, and he blamed it on their sex life becoming stale. After some discussion, Chelsea agreed to spice things up a little bit. Daryl convinced her to watch a few examples with him. Chelsea was uncomfortable but agreed. It seemed exciting for a moment, but Chelsea couldn't help feeling demeaned by the lack of tenderness and romance.

Eventually, Daryl began to make negative comments about her body and recommended they save up for cosmetic surgery. This lowered her self-esteem and made her feel less desirable. No matter how much she tried to please him, it led to her needing to do even more.

One night, Daryl invited another couple over. After a few beers, he suggested they swap mates. Everyone was open to it but Chelsea. Daryl pulled her into another room and mentioned his ongoing sexual frustrations and that he considered cheating. However, instead of sneaking behind her back, he would rather both of them be able to experience having sex with someone else for once. "Besides, is it really cheating if we both give each other permission?" With her self-image in the dumps and not wanting to lose her marriage, Chelsea caved in.

The quality of their marriage didn't improve—it nosedived. She felt even worse. Daryl dove deeper into pornography and suggested they swap sex with other interested people. That's when they both agreed to meet with me. When the assistant brought them into my office, I met two attractive young people. Daryl looked perturbed, and Chelsea had a confused gaze. Initially, they presented to me as just having marital problems, but after I asked a few questions, Chelsea spilled the entire story.

LOVE RENEWED WITH THE TRUTH

In counseling I always ask for the faith background of the individuals so I can be sensitive to their beliefs as well as use it as a means of persuading them toward truth. First, I appealed to Daryl, "You do realize adultery is a violation of military law, right? It's still adultery even if your spouse gives you permission."

Next, I reasoned with Chelsea, "Do you know what the Bible teaches about adultery? In 1 Corinthians 6:9, God warns us not to be deceived, because adulterers will not inherit the kingdom of God." Then I asked both of them if I could share some ancient marital advice from the wisest man who ever lived, King Solomon. They agreed, so I read:

> Drink water from your own well[1]—
>> share your love only with your wife.
> Why spill the water of your springs[2] in the streets,
>> having sex with just anyone?
> You should reserve it for yourselves.
>> Never share it with strangers.
>
> Let your wife be a fountain of blessing for you.
>> Rejoice in the wife of your youth. . . .

1. Here, "well" is a metaphor for the female's sexual anatomy.
2. Here, "springs" is a metaphor for the male's sexual anatomy.

> Let her breasts satisfy you always.
> May you always be captivated by her love.
> Why be captivated, my son, by an immoral woman,
> or fondle the breasts of a promiscuous woman?
> (Prov. 5:15–20 NLT)

At the close of our session, we scheduled a follow-up appointment, then I gave them some resources on recovering from infidelity and restoring trust. With Daryl, I shared the prayer on pornography addiction found in the appendix of this book, and I gave him a special assignment—to compliment his wife's body at least once a day for the next 30 days.[3]

LOVE DISRUPTED BY SOMETHING DEMONIC

The next time I met with Daryl and Chelsea, they had a story to tell. When Daryl left my office, he returned to work. However, Chelsea remained in the parking lot sitting in her car, deeply convicted by the Scriptures I shared with her. "In that very moment, I told God how sorry I was, and I rededicated my life to him," she said.

Daryl chimed in, "Two days later, Chelsea and I were arguing, because she caught me watching pornography. I slipped. I did good for two days, but I just felt it drawing me. Feeling bad that I disappointed her, I picked up the Bible to read it, but all the words on the pages mysteriously disappeared.

---

3. I credit Tommy Nelson for highlighting that King Solomon admired his fiancée's beauty from "head to toe" before marriage (4:1–7) but had to rekindle his interests by admiring her from "toe to head" after marriage (7:1–9). See his video series, *The Song of Solomon: A Study of Love, Sex, Marriage, and Romance* (Dallas: Hudson, 1995).

Then I tried to pray. All of a sudden, something grabbed my neck and started choking me."

Chelsea jumped in before he could finish, "I sensed right away it was something evil. I asked God to help me. Then I remembered the words I used to hear my grandmother say. So I placed my hand on Daryl's arm, and I said, 'I rebuke you in the Name of Jesus!'"

Daryl finished the story, "Immediately, I felt the need to throw up. So I ran to the bathroom, and I vomited a strange, tar-like substance. I sat on the bathroom floor for a moment. Then I stood up and felt lighter. Then I looked at Chelsea and said, 'For the first time in my life, I feel clean!' I haven't had a desire to watch porn ever since."[4]

LOVE WITH CLARITY FROM THE TRUTH

The last time I saw Chelsea and Daryl, they were on cloud nine. Whether you are married or single, these 15 scriptural and psychological facts can help you:

1. Research shows the euphoric feelings of romantic love last only an average of two years.[5]

2. However, those romantic feelings, while no longer automatic, can be rekindled with intentional efforts to meet each spouse's top identified emotional needs.[6]

3. Stats indicate that people who are virgins when they marry have the highest rate of sexual satisfaction in

---

4. Please see the prayer on pornography located in the appendix.

5. Gary Chapman, *Things I Wish I'd Known before We Got Married* (Chicago: Northfield, 2010), 22.

6. Willard F. Harley, *His Needs, Her Needs: Building an Affair-Proof Marriage* (Grand Rapids: Revell, 2001), 19.

their marriages, but those who had previous sexual experience suffer divorce at a rate two times higher.[7] Satan can deceive us into thinking the opposite, thus opening the door to temptation.

4. Satan tempts you where there is unmet desire, and he is banking on your willingness to meet your wants apart from God's will (Matt. 4:2–3).

5. However, God never forbids anything that is truly good for us (James 1:17).

6. Also, God's blessings come with no sorrow attached (Prov. 10:22).

7. "His commandments are not burdensome" (1 John 5:3 NLT); instead, they grant us joy (Ps. 119:111).

8. "How can a young person stay pure? By obeying [God's] word" (Ps. 119:9 NLT). Remember, Jesus replied to every temptation with, "It is written" (Matt. 4:4, 7, 10).

9. If we are praying daily, "Lead us not into temptation," as Jesus commanded (Matt. 6:13; Luke 11:4), then He also expects us to do everything to avoid it (people, places, and things).

10. Pornography is forbidden because Jesus commands us not to look upon others in sexual lust (Matt. 5:28). He wants us to learn how to conquer the inner thoughts that lead to outward sin.

11. If a believer wants to fulfill their sexual urges, they should prayerfully find another believer to marry while keeping the relationship sexually pure until the

7. Chapman, *Things I Wish I'd Known*, 97.

wedding (Song of Sol. 2:7; 3:5; 8:4; 1 Cor. 7:1; 2 Cor. 6:14).

12. Sin twists what God meant as good—drinking becomes drunkenness, eating becomes gluttony, and sexuality becomes sensuality leading to insatiability, where we are tempted to allow anyone or anything to meet our desires in any way, anywhere (Prov. 27:20).

13. Yet God gives us self-control and the desire and ability to obey Him—as we yield to Him (Gal. 5:19–23; Phil. 2:13).

14. This is why we can claim, "I have learned the secret of being content in any and every situation, whether well fed or hungry, whether living in plenty or in want. I can do all this through [Christ] who gives me strength" (Phil. 4:12–13 NIV).

15. "Plans fail for lack of counsel, but with many advisers they succeed" (Prov. 15:22 NIV), so seek advice from qualified people in whatever stage of life you find yourself struggling—whether you are married or single.

Counseling exposed lies Chelsea and Daryl believed about their marriage and themselves. Had they initially sought professional advice, they more than likely would have avoided those regrettable choices. Also, Daryl's effort to repent revealed he was demonized. Nevertheless, it took only an eight-word rebuke from his young bride (who was only two days rededicated to Christ) to free him. Chelsea is a reminder that God's authority to confront demons isn't limited by special skills or spiritual age. All it requires is employing the Name of Jesus.

13

SEXUALLY SEDUCING SPIRITS

From as early as she could remember, Sophie received compliments on her beauty. In middle school, boys fought just to stand next to her in line or sit in the same seat with her on the bus. By the time she reached high school, she was turning heads. She had a boyfriend who responded to her every beck and call. However, she grew bored of him. *Besides*, she thought, *why have just one boyfriend when I can have other girls' boyfriends too?* She developed a desire to see how many men she could seduce—especially men who were in committed relationships.

What prompted Sophie to contact me for counseling? It was a sermon series I preached on sexual purity. I had a young adult congregation growing by leaps and bounds. As any pastor knows, you must be prepared to address everything sheep bring in from the pasture. Young people with raging hormones and countless options contrary to the will of God need clear guidance. Based on my personal journey in this area as a young man, I felt doubly obligated to preach and teach on the subject.

THE SPIRIT OF SEDUCTION HAS A NAME

As soon as Sophie walked into my office, a word flashed in my head like a banner. I shrugged it off and opened our session with prayer. Afterward, Sophie pressed the play button on her heart. "Honestly, I've been very confused lately, since you started your sermon series three weeks ago. Well, there's nothing wrong with your messages. I'm just confused. I don't know why I'm struggling."

Then the word flashed in my head for a second time.

"I grew up in the church," Sophie continued. "Many of my family members are ordained ministers. They even participated in my baptism. I know sex outside marriage is wrong, but I'm confused as to why I can't stop."

I asked more specific questions, and she answered me the best she could. However, our session was ending in a few minutes, and I had another client already in the waiting area. After giving her homework, we bowed our heads to pray. As I was about to speak, the same word flashed in my head for a third time. At this point, I thought to myself, *Is God trying to tell me something?*

After a long pause with our heads bowed, I said, "Sophie, I apologize for the silence, but from the moment you entered my office, this word has appeared in my head three times— even as we bowed to pray. Does it mean anything to you?"

When I said the word, a demon surfaced in her.

She panicked. "I can't see! Now I can't hear! Something is taking over my body, and it wants me to attack you. It's trying to get me to start scratching you!"

In the Name of Jesus, I bound the demon and commanded it to release its hold on her and to give her back the full function of her body. The takeover subsided and her sight and hearing returned. She was trembling in terror as tears washed over her face. Sophie was no longer confused about her seemingly out-of-control seductive desires. The root was an evil spirit. The word that triggered this demonic encounter was *affirmation.*

REVIEWING THE THREE AVENUES OF TEMPTATION

Sophie became demonized when she yielded to the pride of life. Admired for her beauty, she sought to affirm her self-worth by exercising seductive powers over men.

I asked Sophie if she wanted to be free of this evil spirit, and she replied, "Yes!" So I asked her to remain in my office while I spoke with the client in the waiting area. I talked with the client to ensure his need wasn't urgent and explained I had a crisis to address. I apologized for the inconvenience and rescheduled our session.

I returned to my office and journeyed with Sophie through the *Steps to Freedom in Christ.* During this process, she confessed her sins, renounced the sin of seduction, and banished all associated demons from her life.

THE SPIRIT OF SEDUCTION—ORIGINS AND OTHER NAMES

As with all Second Death Sins,[1] seduction is strongly influenced by demons. This is why Jesus, His Apostles, ancient Jews, and early Christians gave serious warnings about the link between unrepentance and demonization.

1. See 1 Cor. 6:9–10; Gal. 5:19–21; Rev. 21:8.

We can trace the activity of sexual demons from the first humans before the flood to victims of the modern day. The first book of the Bible records sex-craving angels taking women and fathering children with them (Gen. 6:1–4). There are historical accounts of victims who continued to suffer attacks from sexual demons in the ancient world. It was even believed there was a possibility that "anyone who sleeps alone in a house will be seized by the evil spirit Lilith."[2]

Who is Lilith?[3] The Bible mentions her only once by name—in Isaiah 34:14, where it references her lurking in a desert wasteland. Historically, she is defined as a female night demon related to sexual life.[4] Most English translations show discomfort with this translation, so they render Lilith as a night animal.[5] However, two versions, the RSV ("night hag") and the NASB ("night monster"), are more accurate in their renderings. Although other ancient civilizations refer to Lilith by different names, they consistently record young men being victimized by her sexual attacks.[6]

Archaeologists verify historical concern about this specific demon. They found prayer bowls buried on the grounds of ancient homes. These bowls were carved with images of

---

2. BT, Shabbat 151b.10.

3. Hebrew: לילית (*Lilith*), "name of a female night-demon" (BDB, 4890).

4. Holladay, 4115.

5. The ESV and KJV refer to her as a night bird or owl, while the NIV, NKJV, and NLT refer to her as a night creature.

6. Daniel Schwemer, "Demons, Demonology," in *The Encyclopedia of the Bible and Its Reception*, vol. 6 of *Dabbesheth—Dreams and Dream Interpretation* (Berlin: de Gruyter, 2012), 535. He also notes, "Together with the male Lilû and the female Lilītu, Ardat-lilî belongs to a family of wind-demons (Sumerian lil, 'breeze, spirit'), and traditions associated with Lilītu, Ardat-lilî and Lamaštu live on in Hebrew Lilith."

Lilith along with a command to ward off her visits. One such bowl reads:

I adjure you, male lili and female lili . . . that you not show yourself to him in the form of a man [or] the form of a woman, nor as a related woman or as an unrelated woman, and do not appear to him in any form, and do not lie down with him, not in a dream of the night nor in a dream of the day.[7]

Notice that a Lilith spirit can reveal itself as male or female. It can also visit a person in their dreams, day or night. These entities were later referred to as "incubus" (male sex-demon) and "succubus" (female sex-demon). Up through the Middle Ages (AD 500–1400), historians validate a continual issue with sexual demons.[8] Even beyond this time period, theologians document people making pacts as sexual partners with these beings.[9]

As recently as 2023, I counseled a young man who had made such a pact. This young man validated how Lilith (or the succubus) would visit him a few nights a week in the form of an old girlfriend. After a while, he grew uncomfortable

7. Bohak, "Expelling Demons and Attracting Demons in Jewish Magical Texts," 180. He adds, "This bowl was first edited by Christa Muller-Kessler, *Die Zauberschalentexte*, 40 (No. 10); it was re-edited in James Nathan Ford and Matthew Morgenstern, *Aramaic Incantation Bowls*, and my translation follows theirs, with minor modifications."

8. Cavan W. Concannon, "The Belief That Demons Have Sex with Humans Runs Deep in Christian and Jewish Traditions," The Conversation, August 12, 2020, https://theconversation.com/the-belief-that-demons-have-sex-with-humans -runs-deep-in-christian-and-jewish-traditions-143589.

9. Charles Zika, "Demons, Demonology," in *The Encyclopedia of the Bible and Its Reception*, vol. 6 of *Dabbesheth—Dreams and Dream Interpretation* (Berlin: de Gruyter, 2012), 564–65. The specific theologians he refers to are Johann Nider and Johannes Tinctor.

with the creepiness of the visits. One night, she appeared and violently mounted him. He stated, "When I told her no, she morphed into a gray, hideous creature, then growled at me through her disgusting teeth!"

THE SPIRIT OF SEDUCTION—STILL ACTIVE

Sadly, this counselee wasn't the only one I counseled on this matter. Today, men and women are still victimized by these sexual spirits,[10] and some people intentionally invoke them. Ancient and current history validate that Satan and his demons not only are interested in influencing humans and watching them engage in forbidden sexual acts but also desire to participate.

I was witnessing to a government contractor named Dre. He was a broad-shouldered weight lifter. I was sharing with him the importance of sexual purity and how demons can take special interest in this Second Death Sin. I still remember his uninterested responses: "Oh really . . . yeah . . . okay."

A few days later, I received an alarming phone call from him. He said, "I went to bed last night after watching that Christian DVD you let me borrow. The next morning, I felt my girlfriend fondling me. I looked over at the clock and said to myself, 'Normally she's gone to work by now.' So I turned over, and she was gone. But to my shock, there was still a hand touching me down there. So I rolled over on my stomach, then I felt the hand reach through the mattress and start touching me again. When I called on Jesus, it stopped."

10. Chavez, "Modern Practice, Archaic Ritual," 19.

In short order, he submitted his life to Christ, journeyed through the *Steps to Freedom in Christ*, and was married a few months later.

THE CHURCH MUST TAKE AN ACTIVE STANCE AGAINST THE SPIRIT OF SEDUCTION

Besides the civil rights movement of the mid-1900s, America's greatest social upheavals are related to sexual revolutions. From a biblical perspective, these movements have eternal ramifications, because Scripture clearly warns that a person cannot inherit the kingdom of God if they practice sexual sins (1 Cor. 6:9–10; Gal. 5:19–21; Rev. 21:8).[11] Of course, this plays right into Satan's agenda, because he sought humanity's eternal doom from the very beginning.

Among other evils, why is Satan interested in sexual immorality? Well, a marriage is consummated by the sexual union of the husband and wife (Gen. 2:24). Also, heterosexual marriage is the foundation of all human societies. More importantly, Christian marriage is the physical picture of the spiritual marriage of Christ and His church (Eph. 5:31–32). Therefore, destroying heterosexual marriage— whether through divorce, extramarital relationships, or unauthorized unions—blurs the image of the Gospel,[12] with severe societal consequences.

Here are some other factors worth considering:

11. See also chap. 1, "The Realm of Darkness Dispelled by the Light," where I share my testimony as well as biblical warnings about sexual immorality as a Second Death Sin.

12. As stated in chap. 5, the Greek word *mystērion* (mystery) is used by the Apostle Paul on most occasions to refer to the unfolding of the Gospel (Rom. 16:25; 1 Cor. 15:51; Eph. 3:3–4; Col. 1:25–27; 1 Tim. 3:16).

1. Sexual sin is the only sin a person can commit against their own body (1 Cor. 6:18).
2. Sexual sin puts you at risk of contracting incurable diseases (Prov. 5:3, 11).
3. Sexual sin joins your spirit, not just your body, to another person (Gen. 2:24; 1 Cor. 6:16).
4. Sex is forbidden with an adulterer (Prov. 6:29–32).
5. Sex is forbidden with a prostitute (Prov. 6:23–26).
6. Sex is forbidden with a promiscuous person (Prov. 5:3, 7–8).
7. Therefore, sex is authorized only with your heterosexual spouse (Gen. 2:24; Prov. 5:15, 17; 1 Cor. 7:2).

Considering the previous chapter on pornography as well as this one on sexual demons, we should clearly see the need to avoid all forbidden sexual sins. If you are personally a victim of a sexual demon, I recommend you reread this chapter and either utilize the practices found within or seek a qualified church leader for help. If you desire protection from such demons, I recommend you begin a daily practice of reciting the Lord's Prayer—especially at the beginning and end of your day.

What's the payoff for sexual purity? The Apostle Paul promises, "If anyone cleanses himself from what is dishonorable, he will be a vessel for honorable use, set apart as holy, useful to the master of the house, ready for every good work" (2 Tim. 2:21). No human pleasure can match the worth of being a vessel of honor, directly used by God in this lifetime and into eternity.

14

PARANORMAL DISTURBANCES

Monday morning the phone rang. I picked up the receiver. "Sir, you have Mr. Phillips on line one." The conversation that followed would lead to an interesting day. The day before, I preached a message from 1 John 4:1: "Beloved, do not believe every spirit, but test the spirits to see whether they are from God, for many false prophets have gone out into the world." I spoke about how early Christians understood this verse to apply to leaders and spirits.

Ron Phillips grew up in the inner city. His neighborhood was bustling with excitement. There was always something going on. You could find good as well as trouble, so you had to keep your head on a swivel and make sure you weren't in the wrong place at the wrong time.

The church he attended was perfect for this raucous community. The choir was lively, and the preaching was inspiring. This is where Ron met an older man in the church who took an interest in him—especially since his parents were divorced and his father was living in another state. No one could replace his dad, but in time he allowed this man to become like a close uncle.

"Uncle Roy" saw that Ron had a good head on his shoulders, and he did everything he could to encourage the young man. He met Ron's mother and obtained permission to take him to local events. They met for lunch regularly and forged a great relationship that lasted through high school graduation. Before Ron headed off to college, Uncle Roy began teaching him other things he could do—besides reading his Bible and praying—to ensure good fortune and to ward off evil. He also gave him a special necklace to wear and sprinkled black powder in his shoes for good luck. Shortly afterward, the paranormal activities began.

GETTING TO THE BOTTOM OF HIS UPPER-LEVEL FOOTSTEPS

By now, Ron and I were ten minutes into our phone call. He said, "Every time I came home from college, Uncle Roy either gave me a new charm or performed some type of spiritual ritual on me. I appreciated his efforts, but by now I was beginning to sense there was something odd and superstitious about these practices that I couldn't find in the Bible."

I asked him to specify what he meant by paranormal activities.

"Something moving in my room," Ron said.

"How long has this been happening?"

"Since college, but it got worse when I moved into this new house."

"Are you married?" I asked.

"No, my fiancée and I split up."

"Do you have a roommate?"

He realized I was asking if someone else could validate his claims. "No, but the footsteps in my attic are starting to keep me up at night."

"Have you inspected your attic?"

"Yes, and it's a new home, and there is no way to enter it from the outside."

"Are you sure it's not an animal?"

"I hear feet."

"What kind of feet?"

"Put it this way," Ron said. "It made one of the ceiling tiles fall down last night."

After asking a few more questions, I realized Ron had a legitimate spiritual issue. Uncle Roy was practicing what is called religious syncretism. He was attempting to synchronize and blend other religious practices with Christianity—in this case, elements of voodoo. I reassured Ron we could resolve his demonic disturbances, and he exclaimed, "Thank God."

Then he asked, "Can you come over to do a house blessing?"

I asked him if he was a believer, and he said, "Yes."

I said, "Great! We share the same authority in Christ over evil spirits. Let me send you a prayer you can utilize, but you'll need to destroy all of Uncle Roy's charms and renounce all of his superstitious teachings." (See the prayers on cleansing a home or room in the appendix.)

Ron emailed me the next day. He was amazed that for the first time in five years there was complete silence throughout the night.

195

SOMETHING EVIL HIDDEN WITHIN

I recently came across the story of a pastor who helped a woman in the same way I assisted Ron. The lady visited a New Age bookstore. She was enamored by a figurine of a beautiful fairy. After purchasing it, she started having paranormal disturbances in her home. She consulted her pastor about the ordeal. During the counseling session, she disclosed her purchase of the figurine.

He instructed her to remove it and all New Age materials from her house. As they were bagging all the items for trash pickup, the figurine broke—coincidentally. To their utter dismay, inside it they discovered another small statue of a headless priest with hands glued to a satanic altar.[1] This is an example of why the Bible warns us that "the secret power of lawlessness is already at work" (2 Thess. 2:7 NIV).

Some demonic encounters can be bizarre, but that never stopped Jesus. One of His most perplexing cases was the demonized man of the Gadarenes who was infested with a legion of evil spirits (Mark 5:1–9; note that a Roman legion contained up to 6,000 soldiers). Jesus expelled all the evil spirits at once, and they went into a herd of 2,000 pigs. The pigs then ran off a cliff and fell to their deaths (5:12–13).

To demonstrate His kingdom in worldwide operation, Christ decided to share His authority with us—enabling us to successfully confront demonic forces that interfere with His peace in our lives (Luke 10:19). As kingdom warriors, let us claim the freedom He secured for us as we continue to advance in His Name.

1. Chavez, "Modern Practice, Archaic Ritual," 9.

15

TESTING THE SPIRITS—
GHOST OR DEMON?

Raymond woke up thirsty in the middle of the night. He slowly rolled out of bed so as not to disturb his sleeping wife, slipped on his robe, quietly walked out of the room, flipped on the stairwell light, and then proceeded downstairs to the refrigerator.

When he was halfway down, a man appeared at the bottom of the stairs and started walking upward. Raymond stopped, rubbed his eyes, blinked a few times, and then opened his eyes real wide to ensure he was seeing clearly. Sure enough, there was another man in the stairwell! By this time, he was two steps away.

Raymond froze. The other man realized his fear, took two more steps, softly grabbed Raymond's forearm, and assured him, "Do not fear. I am a fellow servant of the Lord Jesus Christ sent here to protect your wife." Then he released his arm, continued to walk upstairs, and entered their bedroom. Raymond followed right behind him into the room, but the "man" was nowhere to be found—not in the closet, in the bathroom, or under the bed. Raymond woke his wife and told her everything. However, neither of them ever saw or heard from the "man" again.

THEY ACTUALLY STUDY THIS

Do supernatural encounters like this actually happen? I completed an in-person clinical counseling course entitled "The Psychology of Religious Experience." There were two major conclusions: (1) many people have supernatural encounters (in various degrees) but choose not to share them for fear of not being believed; and (2) those encounters remain real to them whether other people believe them or not. Surprisingly, the Apostles' approach is not to dismiss such claims but to test them:

> Beloved, do not believe every spirit, but test the spirits [to determine] whether they are from God, because many false prophets have gone forth into the world. In this, we continue to know the Spirit of God: every spirit confessing that Jesus Christ has come in the flesh, is of God, and every spirit not confessing Jesus, is not of God; this is that of the antichrist. (1 John 4:1–3, author's translation from Greek)

In other words, if the spiritual source holds true to everything the Apostles teach in the New Testament about Jesus, then it passes the test. Testing spirits is important because the Scriptures warn us to neither be exploited by the devil nor be ignorant of his schemes (2 Cor. 2:11).

After taking that course, I became strategic in my own preaching, teaching, and counseling to address such matters in an effort to expose them to biblical testing. The true stories I share in this book are just a few of the countless ones I've heard and continue to hear.

LET'S TALK ANGELS FOR A MOMENT

To determine whether Raymond's encounter on the stairs is scripturally legitimate, we must review what the Bible teaches about angels. The word *angel* actually means "messenger" and can apply to a human.[1] However, the context or the Bible translation usually makes it clear which is intended. This is why the biblical test applies to either a human or a spirit claiming to be sent by God. The Bible has much to say about angels, but for our study, we will review a few passages from just the New Testament:

1. Angels are created by Christ and for His glory (Col. 1:15–17).
2. Angels worship Christ and encourage us to do the same (Rev. 5:11–12; 14:7; 19:10; 22:9).
3. Angels calm humans, often saying, "Do not fear" (Matt. 28:5; Luke 1:13, 30; 2:10; Rev. 1:17).
4. Angels are ministering spirits sent by God to serve believers (Heb. 1:14);
5. Angels can appear:
   a. in a dream (Matt. 1:20; 2:13, 19–20);
   b. in human form (Heb. 13:2); and

---

1. The Greek word is ἄγγελος (*angelos*), "messenger." The Hebrew equivalent is מלאך (*malak*). Both words can apply to human or supernatural beings. The biblical context usually identifies to which it is referring.

    c. instantly to deliver a message, then disappear
       afterward—the Bible shows them to have no inter-
       est in having ongoing interactions with humans
       (Matt. 28:2–7; Luke 1:11–20, 26–38; Acts 1:10–11;
       5:19–20).

On the other hand, demons, as previously discussed:

1. reject Christ;
2. seek to be worshiped;
3. inflict suffering;
4. can appear as angels of light to deliver a false
   message;
5. tend to revisit the person; and
6. thrive on instilling fear (2 Tim. 1:7).

Let us test Raymond's experience based on these scriptural truths. The spiritual being

1. claimed Jesus as his Lord;
2. implied he is a fellow worshiper of Christ;
3. calmed Raymond;
4. reassured him he was there to protect his wife; and
5. disappeared after sharing the purpose of his visit.

Thus, it meets the scriptural standards of an angel as we discussed.

It may help to know that Raymond's wife was formerly a witch who had recently converted to Christianity. As a result, she was facing increased spiritual warfare. Additionally,

Raymond was thirsty partly because he was in the middle of a multiday fast for her. The night that angel visited was the best night's sleep she had in months—an answer to their prayers.

VISITORS FROM BEYOND THE GRAVE

Maria was devastated about her mother's sudden death. I conducted the midweek funeral, then stood in the foyer on Sunday to ensure I could personally greet her.

Two weeks passed, then Maria came to church wearing a huge smile and laughing out loud with other members—a drastic reversal of emotions. Curious, I requested a meeting with her for grief counseling. A few days later, Maria walked into my office extremely cheerful. Her mother's funeral had been just two weeks earlier, but Maria was acting as though her mother never died. That's when she smiled at me and said, "My mother's ghost visited me last week."

After asking for details, I told Maria, "You do understand there is no such thing as a ghost?"

Maria barked back, "That was my mother!"

Then I opened my Bible to Ecclesiastes 12:6–7 and read when a person dies, "the dust returns to the ground it came from, and the spirit returns to God who gave it" (NIV).

At that, she became furious. "I know that was my momma."

When I realized I wasn't getting anywhere, I asked her to conduct a simple test in accordance with 1 John 4:1–3. "The next time your mother visits you, ask her what she thinks about Jesus." Aiming to prove me wrong, she agreed.

A few days passed and I received a phone call from Maria. She was frantic and requested to see me right away. When she entered my office, she was trembling in fear. I asked her what happened. Maria went on to tell me that after our counseling session, her mother visited her two more times—always in the middle of the night. During the third visit, her mother appeared at the foot of her bed mounted on a white horse and radiating with light. Then her mother announced, "I am now the second highest ranking angel in heaven."

At that point, Maria remembered our agreement. She also thought, *During all three of these visits my mother never mentioned seeing Jesus—she loved Jesus!* So Maria asked, "Mother, what do you think about Jesus?"

Her mother's countenance instantly changed. Her mother's scalp split open, and her skin peeled from the center of her head and fell down to each side of the horse. What now stood before her was the most hideous creature she had ever seen, and it began to blaspheme Christ.

The Apostle Paul warns us, "No one speaking by the Spirit of God will curse Jesus, and no one can say Jesus is Lord, except by the Holy Spirit" (1 Cor. 12:3 NLT). While Raymond's encounter passes the scriptural test above, Maria's experience fails.

The demon masquerading as Maria's dead mother claimed to be an angel but disclosed no apparent purpose from God and kept visiting her. After Maria performed the scriptural test that exposed the deception, the demon never returned.

One of my colleagues, Peter, had a similar experience. A young man was grieving his uncle who recently died. During the session with Peter, the counselee disclosed that his dead uncle recently started visiting him in the middle of the night. A noise would startle him out of his sleep. When he sat up, he would see a waving sheet floating parallel to the ground. It would rise before his bed and assume the image of his uncle.

Peter made it clear, "That is not your uncle!" Upon the counselee's request, Peter agreed to visit his home that Thursday to conduct a house cleansing.

The next morning, Peter received a frantic phone call. It was the young man—delivering a message from the grave. He cautioned Peter, "My uncle visited me last night. This time the sheet was waving violently, and when my uncle appeared, he was angry! He said, 'Tell Peter if he comes here Thursday night, I'm gonna kill him!'"

Upon hearing this, Peter rejoiced and declared, "Challenge accepted!" He conducted the house cleansing, the demon posing as the uncle never returned, and Peter is alive and well many years later.

Did you notice details in the dead uncle's threat? If the uncle was an angel sent by God, why did he feel threatened about Peter praying over the home? Also, how did he know what day he was coming over? Additionally, how did he even know Peter's name? (See Luke 10:19; Acts 19:13–16.)

THE TEST THAT STANDS THE TEST OF TIME

The scriptural test of 1 John 4:1–3 remains historically relevant because the Apostle Paul warns us, "The Spirit clearly says that in later times some will abandon the faith and follow deceiving spirits and things taught by demons" (1 Tim. 4:1 NIV). The last days ("later times") are marked as the period between Jesus's crucifixion and His second coming. This is why the Apostle John alerts us, "Dear children, this is the last hour; and as you have heard that the antichrist is

203

coming, even now many antichrists have come. This is how we know it is the last hour" (1 John 2:18 NIV). Therefore, we are cautioned that—until Jesus returns—demons will impart belief systems that oppose the teachings of Christ.

Numerous messengers throughout history have claimed to be sent by God but were not (1 Kings 13:14–26; 22:22; Gal. 2:4; 2 Pet. 2:1). This is what prompts the Apostle Paul to also add, "But even if we or an angel from heaven should preach a gospel other than the one we preached to you, let them be under God's curse! As we have already said, so now I say again: If anybody is preaching to you a gospel other than what you accepted, let them be under God's curse!" (Gal. 1:8–9 NIV). What does the Bible call a cursed angel? It is a demon.

In Satan's efforts to deceive humanity, he "disguises himself as an angel of light" (2 Cor. 11:14 NLT). He does this because there are numerous examples in the Bible of angelic visits. In the New Testament, an angel visits

1. the Virgin Mary (Luke 1:30–31);
2. her eventual husband, Joseph (Matt. 1:20); and
3. the Apostle John, directing him to write the book of Revelation (Rev. 1:1; 22:16).

Satan tries to emulate holy angels, so it's still necessary for us to test the spirits as well as people who claim to be visited by them.

Since Scripture predicts an increase in unbiblical beliefs taught by demons, I believe it's important for us to view how the scriptural test remains successful throughout the last-days period. Coincidentally, Islam and Mormonism trace their origins to angelic visits, so let's examine them.

In AD 610, Muhammed claimed he was visited in a cave by the Angel Gabriel, who claimed the Bible was corrupted. Then he supernaturally enabled the illiterate Muhammed to write the Qur'an. In it, Jesus is not crucified and is only a prophet—He is not the Son of God as historically taught by the Apostles. True or false: Islam passes the test of 1 John 4:2. False. According to Galatians 1:8–9, this makes it a religion inspired by demons.

In 1823, Joseph Smith (founder of the Church of Jesus Christ of Latter-day Saints, also known as Mormonism) was visited by an angel named Moroni. He told Joseph Smith the church had fallen away from truth, then presented him a new "gospel" on golden plates that became known as the Book of Mormon. In it, Jesus is a god and not God the Son as historically taught by the Apostles. True or false: The Mormon church passes the test of 1 John 4:2. False. Again, according to Galatians 1:8–9, this makes it a religion inspired by demons.

The Apostles warn us further, "We [Christ's apostles] are from God; whoever knows God listens to us; he who is not of God does not listen to us. From this we continue to know the spirit of truth and the spirit of deception" (1 John 4:6, author's translation from Greek). Again, the spiritual source passes the test if it holds true to everything the Apostles teach in the New Testament about Jesus.

DEMONS STRIVE TO TAKE ADVANTAGE OF OUR TRAUMAS

After I experienced a long night of uncontrollable coughing, my wife drove me to the emergency room. The doctor thoroughly examined me and prescribed some antibiotics. This clinic was unusually empty, so the doctor and I began to enjoy some small talk.

When he discovered I was a pastor, he mentioned he was a believer and began to ask me a lot of spiritual questions. He then asked me, "Do you believe in ghosts?"

Before I could answer, he shared that his wife had recently been in a terrible car accident and had to be revived three times. Then he whispered, "Ever since she returned from the other side, she can now communicate with ghosts. Our dog even responds to them."

I told him the Bible teaches there are no such things as ghosts, then recommended he have his wife ask these spirits, "What do you think about Jesus?" Since I was returning home that day from out of state, we tried to swap information. Oddly enough, our phones started malfunctioning. Then none of our pens would write. All of a sudden, an ambulance arrived and he had to go. So I yelled at him to look up my phone number in the patient records. However, I never received a phone call—maybe he forgot my name. Nevertheless, I'm certain if his wife had asked the spirits what they thought about Jesus, she would have been shaken out of her deception, as was Maria.

16

IT WASN'T SCHIZOPHRENIA

I was at home on medical leave due to having shoulder surgery when the phone rang. It was US Navy Chaplain Joseph Johnson. We had met the year before at a military function and were also of the same church denomination. What he shared with me led to one of my most bizarre cases of demonization.

With an exhausted voice, he said, "I've been praying and fasting for two days, and mysteriously your name kept coming to mind. Can I share something with you?" He had no idea of my experiences with demonic occurrences.

Curious, I replied, "Sure, please feel free to share, and I'll do what I can to help."

Three days prior, a group of military men were at a function. Suddenly, Victor attacked one of his fellow soldiers. He was so unnaturally strong it took five men to pull him off the other soldier. When they asked him what prompted his violence, he said, "It wasn't me but the demons inside of me!" Based on this admission, the psychologist diagnosed him as having schizophrenia.

Later that day, Chaplain Johnson decided to meet privately with Victor. The soldier insisted he didn't have schizophrenia. He said he had multiple demons. By his own account, Victor claimed to be demonized by upward of 25 spirits with which he personally interacted. He went on to disclose that (1) he was not a Christian; (2) his upbringing had been in another country; and (3) a powerful witch had placed a spell on his family, resulting in many demonic occurrences.

Chaplain Johnson admitted to me that he didn't have a framework for such experiences, so he just disregarded Victor's claims altogether. After Victor finished talking, Chaplain Johnson asked to pray with him and then placed his hands upon his shoulder. He forgot Victor had warned him earlier in their conversation that prayer and Scripture made the demons surface.

Unexpectedly, Victor roared, and his torso began to unnaturally take the shape of a serpent. Then another voice within him snarled, "Have you come to contend with us?"

Terrified, Chaplain Johnson immediately exclaimed, "No!"

Then Chaplain Johnson ran out of the room, grabbed his phone, and called for those who had escorted Victor to his office to come and retrieve him, "Now!"

After Victor left, Chaplain Johnson said he was so frightened and unprepared for such a supernatural occurrence that he went into the chapel and prayed for over two hours and fasted for nearly three days.

Then he asked, "Have you ever experienced anything like this? Do you think you can help this young man?"

I told him I had experience dealing with demonic matters and that he wasn't out of his mind. Also, I agreed to meet with Victor the following week once I returned to the office from medical leave. We compared our calendars and set a day and time.

A few days prior to our scheduled session, Colossians 2:15 kept surfacing in my mind: "In this way, he [Jesus] disarmed the spiritual rulers and authorities [evil spirits]. He shamed them publicly by his victory over them on the cross" (NLT). It's like when a pastor is preparing a sermon and senses God directing their thoughts to a certain message.

Prior to our session, I told Chaplain Johnson, "If Victor is demonized, then we're safe, because Jesus has given us authority over demons [Luke 10:19]. But if he has schizophrenia, we could be in trouble. So if he doesn't have demons and becomes violent, be prepared to run to the door and call for help."

When Victor arrived, he was tall and muscular. I'm short, and I still had one arm in a sling. We sat down nearly knee-to-knee. I had no fear because I didn't come in my own power, for the Scriptures proclaim, "For the weapons of our warfare are not of the flesh [fists, muscles, and physique] but have divine power to destroy strongholds" (2 Cor. 10:4).

Victor was respectful, and I asked him to tell me his story. For nearly an hour, he shared everything already mentioned. He was distraught about his condition, and I felt pity for him. I then asked for his permission to share my thoughts from a Christian perspective. He agreed. I stated, "If you truly have demons, the Bible declares in Colossians 2:15 that Jesus disarmed them and put them to public shame—"

Before I could finish, he interrupted me with a loud yelp. Chaplain Johnson immediately ran to the door, as we discussed, just in case Victor became violent. In that moment, my tongue felt like it was stuck to the roof of my mouth—I had to gather myself. Just as Chaplain Johnson described earlier, Victor's spine began to pop, contort, and concave. The corners of his lips expanded to his earlobes, revealing an unhuman grin. In the last stage, his torso became serpent-like as we remained almost knee-to-knee.

Then he snarled, "Do you know who we are?"

I told them, "I don't care to know who you are. In the Name of Jesus be silent and give Victor back the control of his body."

He tightened his lips, grimaced, and then reconfigured to his normal form.

It was obvious to me that Victor wasn't suffering from schizophrenia. I compassionately reassured him of this. However, I explained to him that expelling the demons without his submission to the Lordship of Jesus Christ would put him at risk for a worse condition. As Jesus taught:

> When an impure spirit comes out of a person, it goes through arid places seeking rest and does not find it. Then it says, "I will return to the house I left." When it arrives, it finds the house unoccupied, swept clean and put in order. Then it goes and takes with it seven other spirits more wicked than itself, and they go in and live there. And the final condition of that person is worse than the first. (Matt. 12:43–45 NIV)

When we submit to the Lordship of Jesus Christ, God indwells us with His Holy Spirit and grants us authority over evil spirits (Luke 10:19; 1 Cor. 6:19). So I emphasized gaining a true knowledge of Jesus was of utmost importance.

As I continued speaking to Victor, I noticed his eyebrows moving as though he was listening to someone else. So I asked him what was going on. He told me the spirits were telling him they wanted to know more about Jesus too.

I responded, "They are lying to you and are only trying to gain your trust."[1]

Instantly, they surfaced like before, and again they threatened, "Do you know who we are?"

Again, I commanded them to be silent and not to say another word to me. He tightened his lips and grimaced. Then I commanded them to give Victor back control of his body. Again, he reconfigured like a robot to his normal form.

Feeling very grieved by his condition, I told Victor I could do something safer, since he wasn't a Christian. I asked if he would allow me to render a blessing over him to keep the spirits bound and at bay within him while God granted him ample time to research who Jesus truly is. I added, if he discovered Jesus to be the Christ, then he could submit to His Lordship, and those evil spirits could be expelled—without the risk of a stronger redemonization. He agreed. However, when I raised my right hand to bless him, he fell over into his lap like a dead man with his arms dangling on both sides of him. I realized the demons rendered him unconscious to prevent him from accepting the blessing, because "faith comes by hearing" (Rom. 10:17 NKJV).

---

1. "Who is the liar? It is whoever denies that Jesus is the Christ. Such a person is the antichrist—denying the Father and the Son" (1 John 2:22 NIV).

I commanded the evil spirits in the Name of Jesus to release Victor and give him back his consciousness. In that second, it was like someone flipped a switch. He awoke and his torso rose back into a fully seated position. Again, I raised my hand to bless him, and he began to cry. Afterward, he said it was the best he felt in years and he was happy for the session. As Chaplain Johnson called for his military assistants, Victor and I exchanged contact information with the plan to regularly talk and email each other as he researched the Christian faith.

As Victor was walking away to get into the military van, I felt the need to stop him and ask, "Why were you crying when I gave you the blessing?"

He responded, "Sir, it wasn't me crying—it was the demons." At that moment, I was reminded of the time Jesus approached the severely demonized man, and the evil spirits bemoaned the probability of being tortured and expelled by him (Luke 8:27–28, 31).

For several weeks, Victor and I communicated regularly. One evening, we were talking on the phone, and he was trying to understand why Jesus had to die on the cross. When I quoted 1 John 1:7 (". . . the blood of Jesus his Son cleanses us from all sin"), Victor yelled out something in a foreign language. Simultaneously, a power surge temporarily blackened our home.

I asked him what happened, and he told me the demons shouted, "Free us!" They could sense their hold on Victor was at risk as he began to learn more about the Gospel of freedom (Gal. 5:1).

I wish I could share that Victor came into a true knowledge of Jesus, submitted to His Lordship, and was freed from those demons. However, the military discharged him, and I lost track of him.

The encounter with Victor was so bizarre that I am glad Chaplain Johnson gave me permission to include his name in this chapter. Neither of us grew up in churches—or even had seminary classes—where we were taught that occurrences like these are real and how to provide pastoral care when they happen.

In closing, I leave you with three conclusions. First, as a priority, we should seek to lead a willing person to faith and repentance in Christ *before* we strive to expel a demon from them. Otherwise, we can place them at risk for redemonization by demons much stronger than the first—especially if the person doesn't subsequently submit to the Lordship of Jesus Christ (Matt. 12:43–45).[2]

Also, the Apostle John teaches that the unbelieving "world is under the control of the evil one" (1 John 5:19 NIV). For us to truly be freed from evil spirits, Scripture requires us to "submit yourselves therefore to God. Resist the devil, and he will flee from you" (James 4:7). Satan's power is limited, but he exercises a level of control over unbelievers, because they are not submitted to the Lordship of Jesus Christ whether due to deception, an unwillingness to change, or not yet hearing the Gospel.

2. In Acts 16:16–19, a fortune teller keeps annoying the Apostle Paul, so he expels a demon from her. Thus, he demonstrates it is possible to expel a demon from an unbeliever. However, without their subsequent repentance, they remain vulnerable to redemonization, according to Jesus (Matt. 12:43–45). I've had cases where a person strove to make a profession of faith, but a demon surfaced and interfered. I bound the evil spirit in the Name of Christ, commanded it to stop, and resumed with the person's submission to Christ, then we confronted the demon accordingly. (See chap. 8, "Confronting Demons through Repentance.")

For clarity, this doesn't mean Satan owns their soul. A person cannot sell their soul to the devil, because God declares, "All souls are mine" (Ezek. 18:4). That includes Satan's own soul. He is an angel created by God who rebelled, and his final day of doom will come at the end of days: "And the devil, who deceived them, was thrown into the lake of burning sulfur, where the beast and the false prophet had been thrown. They will be tormented day and night for ever and ever" (Rev. 20:10 NIV).

Second, we shouldn't take for granted the ancient biblical practice of raising our hands to bless people. The Scriptures teach:

1. When inaugurated as Israel's first high priest, "Aaron lifted his hands toward the people and blessed them" (Lev. 9:22 NIV).

2. As Jesus prepared to ascend back into heaven, "He lifted up his hands and blessed [the disciples]" (Luke 24:50 NIV).

This practice is so significant that we see it initiated by the first high priest under the Old Covenant, then repeated by the new High Priest under the New Covenant.

Sadly, I've visited many modern churches, and the benediction at the end of the service, which is a blessing of the people, is disregarded entirely. In addition to knowing the authority we have in Christ to confront evil spirits, I pray you are inspired by the actual account in this chapter to resume the powerful practice of blessing others.

Third, it can be exhilarating to witness Christ's power when we successfully confront a demon in His Name.

214

However, we cannot let it distract us from our highest priority: continual submission to the Lordship of Jesus Christ. As Jesus Himself warns, "Do not rejoice that the spirits submit to you, but rejoice that your names are written in heaven" (Luke 10:20 NIV).

17

LOST, TRAPPED, AND DYING IN A VEGETATIVE STATE

Sometimes during a truth encounter, I feel like a detective in a crime show. As I lead the interview, the person is shocked when I reveal the presence of an undercover agent. Likewise, deception is Satan's most effective tactic because we don't know when we are being deceived—until it is revealed. It has worked on all humans since our creation. This is why Jesus declares:

> He [the devil] was a murderer from the beginning, and does not stand in the truth, because there is no truth in him. When he lies, he speaks out of his own character, for he is a liar and the father of lies. (John 8:44)

His goal is to mislead people into rejecting the Gospel. As the Apostle Paul proclaims:

> And even if our gospel is veiled, it is veiled to those who are perishing. The god of this age [Satan] has blinded the minds

216

of unbelievers, so that they cannot see the light of the gospel. (2 Cor. 4:3–4 NIV)

The word *gospel* means "good news," but why is it such?

By this gospel you are saved . . . that Christ died for our sins according to the Scriptures, that he was buried, that he was raised on the third day according to the Scriptures. (1 Cor. 15:2–4 NIV)

Moreover, the Gospel is chiefly important because "the reason the Son of God appeared was to destroy the works of the devil" (1 John 3:8). How did Jesus accomplish this?

He canceled the record of the charges against us [due to our sins] and took it away by nailing it to the cross. In this way, he disarmed [Satan and his demons]. He shamed them publicly by his victory over them on the cross. (Col. 2:14–15 NLT)

Unlike the previous supernatural encounters, I will present an example of how God counteracted one of Satan's efforts by miraculously raising a man out of his vegetative state just hours before his death, then granting him a final chance to submit to Christ and receive eternal life.

One of the realities many military chaplains dread is being promoted into the senior ranks and steadily moving away from actual ministry into administration. One day, while serving as a senior chaplain with a sizable staff, my duties were disrupted. Beforehand, I had cleared my calendar to complete a substantial amount of paperwork that was due that week. My phone rang. After several rings, I begrudgingly placed a bookmark in my thoughts and answered it.

The chaplain assistant on the other end stated, "Chaplain Dabbs, a nurse from the ICU is on the other line. They need you at the hospital." The rest of the conversation went like this:

"Where's the hospital chaplain?" I asked.

"Sir, he's on leave."

"What about the other hospital chaplain?"

"Sir, she's deployed."

"Oh, I forgot that. What about the other chaplains?"

"Sir, they are conducting counseling sessions."

"What about the on-call chaplain?"

"Sir, he's at an official function."

"Okay, so what time does the hospital need me to be there?"

"Sir, the nurse asked if you could come as soon as possible."

"Okay, tell her I will be there in a few minutes."

"Yes sir, I will inform her now."

That's when I remembered other times in my ministry when coincidentally I was the only one available to provide care to someone in need. It was typically a divine appointment.

Not knowing what to expect, I prayed, logged out of my computer, jumped into my car, drove a few miles to the hospital, found a parking spot, maneuvered through the maze of cars, climbed a flight of stairs, got into the elevator, went up a number of floors, and walked into the ICU.

As soon as I stepped through the double doors, the nurse met me holding a specialized gown for me to put on. Afterward, she led me to the sink to wash my hands. While I was drying my hands, she asked, "Sir, do you know why you are here?"

When she realized I was clueless, she pointed to one of the rooms and informed me, "The man in that room is a veteran. He lapsed into a vegetative state a few days ago, and the doctors predict he only has 48 hours to live. His daughter arrived yesterday, and today she asked for a chaplain."

When I walked into the room, I saw a lady in business attire pacing the floor and cupping her chin like she was trying to decipher the code to a complex problem. I introduced myself, and she told me her name. After a brief pause, Rhonda said, "My daddy was a mean man. My mother left him, and my brother wants nothing to do with him. I'm a Christian, and I have tried many times to share the Gospel with him, but he made it very clear to me he wants nothing to do with God."

Then she fought back tears as she cried, "The doctors told me he has two days to live. This is my second day being here, and he hasn't even looked at me. I'm afraid for his soul."

Then Rhonda looked over at her father, Charles. I was so attentive to her concerns that I never fully noticed how grave Charles's condition was. He was in a vegetative state staring blankly at the ceiling with tubes running down his throat as he labored to breathe. Both of his hands were strapped to the bed rails pulled up on each side of him.

I sensed Rhonda only wanted a word of encouragement, since her father was unresponsive and literally on his deathbed. In that moment, I felt God peacefully nudge me to quote this Scripture: "The Lord is . . . not willing that any should perish but that all should come to repentance" (2 Pet. 3:9 NKJV).

Then I asked her, "Do you believe this?"

She nodded.

So I motioned for her to join me at the foot of his bed, and I uttered this simple prayer: "Heavenly Father, I come to You on behalf of Your precious daughter. She's concerned about the condition of her father's soul. We were told he has only two days to live, but You hold the power of life and death in Your hands. You declared it's Your desire that no one perishes but that all come to repentance. Therefore, we humbly ask You to give her daddy back his consciousness so that he can make his peace with You. In Jesus's Name. Amen."

Immediately, her father woke up.

Rhonda panicked and quickly backed into the corner of the room screaming, "Oh my God!"

Charles started trembling in terror as he noticed his hands tied to the bed rails and all the tubes coming out of his mouth. I calmly told him, "Sir, I'm Chaplain Dabbs. Your daughter asked me to come here because you've been in a vegetative state for a few days, and the doctors predict you only have 48 hours to live. Would you like to make your peace with God before you die? If so, blink once for 'yes.'"

He looked at Rhonda for a moment, back at me, then blinked once for "yes." I took a moment to explain the Gospel to him and asked him to blink once if he wanted to accept Jesus Christ as his Lord, and he did. Since he could not pray,

I prayed on his behalf, then again asked him to blink once for "amen"—which he did.

As I was departing the room, I saw Rhonda standing beside her father's bed with her hand on his arm as he looked tenderly into her eyes—the first time he was able to do so in those two days. The next morning, I was busy again with paperwork when my phone rang. It was Rhonda. She informed me her father died that very night.

In the scheme of spiritual warfare, I'm sure Satan and his demons celebrated a premature victory—having deceived Charles into hating God all the way to his last day on earth. The man was in a vegetative state and on his deathbed, and the eternal condition of his soul was literally grave—for this life and the afterlife. But God, in His great love, invaded the scene and snatched victory out of the jaws of defeat!

As the Scriptures declare, "There is no wisdom, no insight, no plan that can succeed against the LORD" (Prov. 21:30 NIV).

SPECIAL PRAYERS & DECISIONS FOR SPECIFIC SITUATIONS

SHARED WITH PERMISSION FROM DR. NEIL T. ANDERSON

The following prayers will enhance your growth process and help you make critical decisions. On their own they are unlikely to bring complete resolution or recovery, but they are an excellent starting point. You will then need to work on renewing your mind. Please don't hesitate to seek godly counsel for additional help when needed.

1. Abortion
2. Anxiety
3. Fear
4. Bigotry
5. Cleansing Home/Apartment/Room
6. Living in a Non-Christian Environment
7. Drivenness and Perfectionism
8. Eating Disorders or Self-Mutilation
9. Gambling
10. Gender Identity
11. Homosexuality
12. Marriage
13. Divorce
14. Pornography
15. Substance Abuse
16. Suicidal Tendencies

1. Abortion: Dear Heavenly Father, I confess that I was not a proper guardian and keeper of the life You entrusted to me, and I confess that I have sinned. Thank You that because of Your forgiveness, I can forgive myself. I commit the child to You for all eternity and believe that they are in Your caring hands. In Jesus's name I pray. Amen.

2. Anxiety: Dear Heavenly Father, I am Your child bought by the blood of the Lord Jesus Christ. I am completely dependent on You, and I need You. I know that without Jesus I can't do anything. You know the thoughts and intentions of my heart, and You know my situation from the beginning to the end. I feel as though I am double-minded, and I need Your peace to guard my heart and my mind. I humble myself before You and choose to trust You to exalt me at the right time in any way You choose. I trust You to meet all my needs according to Your riches in glory in Christ Jesus and to guide me into all truth. Please guide me so that I can fulfill my calling to live a responsible life by faith in the power of Your Holy Spirit. "Search me, O God, and know my heart; try me and know my anxious thoughts; and see if there be any hurtful way in me, and lead me in the everlasting way" (Ps. 139:23–24 NASB). In Jesus's precious name. Amen.

3. Fear: Dear Heavenly Father, I confess that I have allowed fear to control my life. Thank You for Your forgiveness. I choose to believe that You have not given me a spirit of fear, but of power, love, and self-control (2 Tim. 1:7). I renounce any spirit of fear operating in my life. I desire to live by faith according to what You have said is true in the power of the Holy Spirit. In Jesus's name I pray. Amen.

4. Bigotry: Dear Heavenly Father, You have created all humanity in Your image. I confess that I have judged others by the color of their skin, their national origin, their social or economic status, their cultural differences, or their sexual orientation. I renounce racism, elitism, and sexism. I choose to believe "there is neither Jew nor Greek, there is neither slave nor free, there is neither male nor female, for you are all one in Christ Jesus" (Gal. 3:28 NASB). Please show me the roots of my own bigotry that I may confess it and be cleansed from such defilement. I pledge myself "to walk in a manner worthy of the calling to which [I] have been called, with all humility and gentleness, with patience, bearing with one another in love, eager to maintain the unity of the Spirit in the bond of peace" (Eph. 4:1–3). In Jesus's name I pray. Amen.

5. For Cleansing Home/Apartment/Room (*After removing and destroying all objects of false worship, pray this prayer aloud—in every room if necessary*): Heavenly Father, I acknowledge that You are the Lord of heaven and earth. In Your sovereign power and love, You have given me all things to enjoy. Thank You for this place to live. I claim my home as a place of spiritual safety for me and my family, and ask for Your protection from all the attacks of the enemy. As a child of God, raised up and seated with Christ in the heavenly places, I command every evil spirit claiming ground in this place, based on the activities of past or present occupants, including me, to leave and never return. I renounce all curses and spells directed against this place. I ask You, Heavenly Father, to post Your holy, warring angels around this place to guard it from any and all attempts of the enemy to enter and disturb Your purposes for me and my family. Thank You, Lord, for doing this in the name of the Lord Jesus Christ. Amen.

6. For Living in a Non-Christian Environment (*After removing and destroying all objects of false worship from your possession, pray this aloud in the place where you live*): Thank You, Heavenly Father, for a place to live and to be renewed by sleep. I ask You to set aside my room [or portion of this room] as a place of spiritual safety for me. I renounce any allegiance given to false gods or spirits by other occupants. I renounce any claim to this room [space] by Satan based on the activities of past or present occupants, including me. On the basis of my position as a child of God and joint heir with Christ, who has all authority in heaven and on earth, I command all evil spirits to leave this place and never return. I ask You, Heavenly Father, to station Your holy, warring angels to protect me while I live here. In Jesus's mighty name I pray. Amen.

7. Drivenness and Perfectionism: Dear Heavenly Father, I renounce the lie that my sense of worth is dependent on my ability to perform. I announce the truth that my identity and my sense of worth are found in who I am as Your child. I renounce seeking the approval and acceptance of other people, and I choose to believe that I am already approved and accepted in Christ because of His death and resurrection for me. I choose to believe the truth that I have been saved not by deeds done in righteousness but according to Your mercy. I choose to believe that I am no longer under the curse of the law because Christ became a curse for me. I receive the free gift of life in Christ and choose to abide in Him. I renounce striving for perfection by living under the law. By Your grace, Heavenly Father, I choose from this day forward to walk by faith in the power of Your Holy Spirit according to what You have said is true. In Jesus's name I pray. Amen.

8. Eating Disorders or Self-Mutilation: Dear Heavenly Father, I renounce the lie that my value as a person is dependent on my appearance or performance. I renounce cutting or abusing myself, vomiting, using laxatives, or starving myself as a means of being in control, altering my appearance, or trying to cleanse myself of evil. I announce that only the blood of the Lord Jesus Christ cleanses me from sin. I realize I have been bought with a price and my body, the temple of the Holy Spirit, belongs to God. Therefore, I choose to glorify God in my body. I renounce the lie that I am evil or that any part of my body is evil. Thank You that You accept me just the way I am in Christ. In Jesus's name I pray. Amen.

9. Gambling: Dear Heavenly Father, I confess that I have been a poor steward of the financial resources that have been in my possession. I have gambled away my future chasing a false god. I have not been content with food and clothing, and the love of money has driven me to behave irrationally and sinfully. I renounce making provision for my flesh in regard to this lust. I commit myself to stay away from all gambling casinos, gambling websites, bookmakers, and lottery sales. I choose to believe that I am alive in Christ and dead to sin. Fill me with Your Holy Spirit so that I don't carry out the desires of the flesh. Show me the way of escape when I am tempted to return to my addictive behaviors. I stand against all of Satan's accusations, temptations, and deceptions by putting on the armor of God and standing firm in my faith. I choose to believe that You will meet all my needs according to Your riches in glory. In Jesus's name I pray. Amen.

10. Gender Identity: Dear Heavenly Father, I choose to believe that You have created all humanity to be either male or female (Gen. 1:27) and commanded us to maintain a distinction between the two genders (Deut. 22:5; Rom. 1:24–29). I confess that I have been influenced by the social pressures of this fallen world and the lies of Satan to question my biological gender identity and that of others. I renounce all the accusations and lies of Satan that would seek to convince me that I am somebody other than who You created me to be. I choose to believe and accept my biological gender identity, and I pray that You would heal my damaged emotions and enable me to be transformed by the renewing of my mind. I take up the full armor of God (Eph. 6:13) and the shield of faith to extinguish all the temptations and accusations of the evil one (Eph. 6:16). I renounce any identities and labels that derive from my old nature, and I choose to believe that I am a New Creation in Christ. In the wonderful name of Jesus I pray. Amen.

11. Homosexuality: Dear Heavenly Father, I renounce the lie that You have created me or anyone else to be gay or lesbian, and I agree that in Your Word You clearly forbid homosexual behavior. I choose to accept myself as a child of God, and I thank You that You created me as a man [or woman]. I renounce all homosexual thoughts, urges, drives, and acts, and I renounce all ways that Satan has used these things to pervert my relationships. I announce that I am free in Christ to relate to the opposite sex and my own sex in the way that You intended. In Jesus's name I pray. Amen.

12. Marriage: Dear Heavenly Father, I choose to believe that You created us male and female, and that marriage is a spiritual bond between one man and one woman who become one in Christ. I believe that bond only can be broken by death, adultery, or desertion by an unbelieving spouse. I choose to stay committed to my vows and to remain faithful to my spouse until physical death separates us. Give me the grace to be the spouse You created me to be, and enable me to love and respect my partner in marriage. I will seek to change only myself and accept my spouse as You have accepted me. Teach me how to speak the truth in love, to be merciful as You have been merciful to me, and to forgive as You have forgiven me. In Jesus's name I pray. Amen.

13. Divorce: Dear Heavenly Father, I have not been the spouse You created me to be, and I deeply regret that my marriage has failed. I choose to believe that You still love and accept me. I choose to believe that I am still Your child, and that Your desire for me is that I continue serving You and others in Your kingdom. Give me the grace to overcome the disappointment and the emotional scars that I carry, and I ask the same for my ex-spouse. I choose to forgive him/her and I choose to forgive myself for all the ways I contributed to the divorce. Enable me to learn from my mistakes and guide me so that I don't repeat the same old-flesh patterns. I choose to believe the truth that I am still accepted, secure, and significant in Christ. Please guide me to healthy relationships in Your church, and keep me from seeking a marriage on the rebound. I trust You to supply all my needs in the future, and I commit myself to follow You. In Jesus's name I pray. Amen.

14. Pornography: Dear Heavenly Father, I confess that I have looked at sexually suggestive and pornographic material for the purpose of stimulating myself sexually. I have attempted to satisfy my lustful desires and polluted my body, soul, and spirit. Thank You for cleansing me and for Your forgiveness. I renounce any satanic bonds I have allowed in my life through the unrighteous use of my body and mind. Lord, I commit myself to destroy any objects in my possession that I have used for sexual stimulation and to turn away from all media that are associated with my sexual sin. I commit myself to the renewing of my mind and to thinking pure thoughts. Fill me with Your Holy Spirit so that I may not carry out the desires of the flesh. In Jesus's name I pray. Amen.

15. Substance Abuse: Dear Heavenly Father, I confess that I have misused substances [alcohol, tobacco, food, prescription or street drugs] for the purpose of pleasure, to escape reality, or to cope with difficult problems. I confess that I have abused my body and programmed my mind in harmful ways. I have quenched the Holy Spirit as well. Thank You for Your forgiveness. I renounce any satanic connection or influence in my life through my misuse of food or chemicals. I cast my anxieties on Christ, who loves me. I commit myself to yield no longer to substance abuse, but instead I choose to allow the Holy Spirit to direct and empower me. In Jesus's name I pray. Amen.

16. Suicidal Tendencies: Dear Heavenly Father, I renounce all suicidal thoughts and any attempts I've made to take my own life or in any way injure myself. I renounce the lie that life is hopeless and that I can find peace and freedom by taking my own life. Satan is a thief and comes to steal, kill, and destroy. I choose life in Christ, who said He came to give me life and give it abundantly (John 10:10). Thank You for Your forgiveness that allows me to forgive myself. I choose to believe that there is always hope in Christ and that my Heavenly Father loves me. In Jesus's name I pray. Amen.

ACKNOWLEDGMENTS

I utter a simple prayer every day: "Lord, make Your will obvious, undeniable, and unavoidable, that I may bump into it, then walk within it accordingly, and may I not miss Your timing!"

Accordingly, this book journey started with a "crazy-pants" idea from Megan Brown—a young lady I mentored in military ministry who's now a three-time author and publishing editor. Meg invited my wife, Octavia, and me to attend a writers' conference—on four days' notice! She covered my plane tickets, conference fees, and meals.

The day prior, Warren and Karen Wilson—leaders who served under one of my previous ministries—spontaneously sent us a love offering that providentially covered Octavia's plane tickets.

At the conference, I met my book agent, Dan Balow. When I told him I wanted to write a book on demons, he tilted his head, looked away for a moment, looked back at me, and replied, "Well, that's a controversial issue. Do you have other topics?" But he sent my proposal to a host of publishers, and a month later, Baker Books offered us a contract.

When I reached out to endorsers, I contacted a spiritual

hero to many, Dr. Neil T. Anderson, whose research—since my college days—filled the gaps of my misunderstandings on spiritual warfare. He read my sample chapters over a weekend and was "all in."

I was also privileged to borrow from the sanctified Harvard mind of Dr. Jeffrey J. Niehaus. He's not only my beloved Hebrew professor but also a respected scholar and successful practitioner of deliverance ministry. I can still hear him asking me, "Is that conclusive?"

Additionally, my spiritual father, Dr. Hobert K. Farrell, joined in. Ever since I was a Bible college student, he taught me, "Keep your finger on the text." His expert instruction in Greek and biblical studies set me on an eventual course to write this book a long time ago.

I also felt I needed feedback from a trusted leader who's still in the trenches of pastoral care. So I sent the manuscript to Dr. Anthony L. Wiggins. Having mentored him from his first sermon through his journey as a senior military chaplain, I knew him to be a faithful expositor of the Scriptures, so when he responded, "This book hits the mark!" I was finally satisfied.

I owe the title of this book to my best friend, bride, and harshest critic, Octavia Dabbs. Her continual love, support, patience, and added vision enabled me to complete this project undeterred.

In addition to those mentioned above, I'm grateful to my beta readers, my contributors, and the Baker Books editors who strove to make this project as perfect as possible for the readers.

God ensured I bumped into all of you at the right time. Like me, you're all a part of His divine plan to aid those suffering in the spiritual war.

BIBLIOGRAPHY

Anderson, Craig. "Violent Music Lyrics Increase Aggressive Thoughts and Feelings." American Psychological Association, 2003. https://www.apa.org/news/press/releases/2003/05/violent-songs.

Anderson, Neil T. *The Bondage Breaker*. Eugene, OR: Harvest House, 2000.

———. *The Bondage Breaker*. Rev. and exp. ed. Eugene, OR: Harvest House, 2019.

———. *The Bondage Breaker—The Next Step*. Eugene, OR: Harvest House, 2011.

Bauer, Walter. *A Greek-English Lexicon of the New Testament and Other Early Christian Literature*. 3rd ed. Edited by Frederick W. Danker. Chicago: University of Chicago Press, 2000.

Bohak, Gideon. "Conceptualizing Demons in Late Antique Judaism." In *Demons and Illness from Antiquity to the Early-Modern Period*, edited by Catherine Rider and Siam Bhayro, 111–12, 128–30. Leiden: Brill, 2017.

———."Demons, Demonology." In *The Encyclopedia of the Bible and Its Reception*. Vol. 6 of *Dabbesheth—Dreams and Dream Interpretation*. Berlin: de Gruyter, 2012.

———. "Expelling Demons and Attracting Demons in Jewish Magical Texts." In *Experiencing the Beyond: Intercultural Approaches*, edited by Gert Melville and Carlos Ruta, 171–72, 179–80. Berlin: de Gruyter, 2018.

————. "Jewish Exorcisms Before and After the Destruction of the Second Temple." In *Was 70 CE a Watershed in Jewish History? On Jews and Judaism Before and After the Destruction of the Second Temple*, edited by Daniel S. Schwartz and Zeev Weiss, 280–84, 290, 299. Leiden: Brill, 2012.

Brown, Francis, S. R. Driver, and Charles A. Briggs. *Hebrew-Aramaic and English Lexicon of the Old Testament* (abridged BDB-Gesenius Lexicon). Ontario: Online Bible Foundation, 1997.

Brown, Michael G. "Why Pray the Lord's Prayer?" *The Banner of Truth* (2007). Accessed January 18, 2024. https://www.christian studylibrary.org/article/why-pray-lord%E2%80%99s-prayer.

Caciola, Nancy. "Exorcism." In *Encyclopedia of Religion*. 2nd ed. Detroit: Macmillan Reference, 2005.

Chavez, William S. "Modern Practice, Archaic Ritual: Catholic Exorcism in America." *Religions* 12, no. 10 (September 2021). https://www.mdpi.com/2077-1444/12/10/811.

Clines, David J. A., ed. *Dictionary of Classical Hebrew*. Vol. 4. Sheffield: Sheffield Academic Press, 1998.

Concannon, Cavan W. "The Belief That Demons Have Sex with Humans Runs Deep in Christian and Jewish Traditions." The Conversation, August 12, 2020. https://theconversation.com/the-belief-that -demons-have-sex-with-humans-runs-deep-in-christian-and-jewish -traditions-143589.

Cost, Ben. "28 Girls Hospitalized with 'Anxiety' after Playing with Ouija Board." *New York Post*, March 7, 2023.

DeLong, William. "Inside the Harrowing Exorcism of Roland Doe, the True Story Behind 'The Exorcist.'" *All That's Interesting*, October 5, 2021. https://allthatsinteresting.com/roland-doe-the-exorcist-true -story.

Dickason, C. Fred. *Demon Possession & the Christian*. Wheaton: Crossway, 1987.

Edersheim, Alfred. *The Life and Times of Jesus the Messiah*. Vol. 1. Peabody, MA: Hendrickson, 1995.

Ekirch, Roger. "Sleep We Have Lost: Pre-Industrial Slumber in the British Isles." *The American Historical Review* 106, no. 2 (April 2001): 357, 366–67, 370–71, 383.

Ensign, Grayson H., and Edward Howe. *Bothered? Bewildered? Bewitched? Your Guide to Practical Supernatural Healing.* Cincinnati: Recovery Publications, 1984.

Erickson, Millard J. *Christian Theology.* Grand Rapids: Baker Books, 1985.

Evans, Craig A. "Jesus and Psalm 91 in Light of the Exorcism Scrolls." In *Celebrating the Dead Sea Scrolls*, edited by Peter W. Flint, Jean Duhaime, and Kyung S. Baek, 548–49, 554. Leiden: Brill, 2012.

Fee, Gordon D. *New Testament Exegesis.* Rev. ed. Louisville: Westminster John Knox, 1993.

Friberg, Timothy, Barbara Friberg, and Neva F. Miller. *Analytical Lexicon to the Greek New Testament.* Grand Rapids: Baker Books, 2000.

Gallagher, Richard. "As a Psychiatrist, I Diagnose Mental Illness. Also, I Help Spot Demon Possession." *Washington Post*, July 1, 2016.

Gentry, Peter J. "Kingdom through Covenant: Humanity as the Divine Image." *Southern Baptist Journal of Theology* 12, no. 1 (Spring 2008): 23.

Gifford, Edwin Hamilton. *Nicene and Post-Nicene Fathers, Second Series.* Vol. 7. Edited by Philip Schaff and Henry Wace. Buffalo: Christian Literature Publishing Co., 1894.

Grudem, Wayne. *Systematic Theology.* Grand Rapids: Zondervan, 1994.

Heiser, Michael S. *Demons.* Bellingham, WA: Lexham Press, 2020.

Hogue, Rodney. "I Was a Christian . . . with a Demon!" *Supernatural Stories*, May 19, 2020. https://www.youtube.com /watch?v=VE3FfhQgDPM.

Holladay, William L. *A Concise Hebrew and Aramaic Lexicon of the Old Testament: Based upon the Lexical Work of Ludwig Koehler and Walter Baumgartner.* Leiden: Brill, 2000.

Jacobs, A. J. "Why Thankfulness and Gratitude Are Jewish Emotions." *Forward*, November 20, 2018. https://forward.com/culture /414468/why-thankfulness-and-gratitude-are-jewish-emotions/.

Jansons, Linards. "Baptismal Exorcism: An Exercise in Liturgical Theology." *Lutheran Theological Journal* 45, no. 3 (2011): 185.

Ken, Thomas. *A Manual of Prayers for the Use of the Scholars of Winchester College*. London: John Martyn, 1675.

Koch, Kurt. *Occult Bondage and Deliverance*. Grand Rapids: Kregel, 1970.

Korn, Eugene, ed. "Noahide Covenant: Theology and Jewish Law Text." Boston College Center for Christian-Jewish Learning. Accessed April 7, 2023. https://www.bc.edu/content/dam/files/research_sites/cjl/texts/cjrelations/resources/sourcebook/Noahide_covenant.htm.

Laycock, Joseph. "Demons, Demonology." In *The Encyclopedia of the Bible and Its Reception*. Vol. 6 of *Dabbesheth—Dreams and Dream Interpretation*. Berlin: de Gruyter, 2012.

Levene, Dan. *A Corpus of Magic Bowls: Incantation Texts in Jewish Aramaic from Late Antiquity*. London: Kegan Paul, 2003.

Lizorkin-Eyzenberg, Eliyahu. "What Does Prayer Mean in Hebrew?" Israel Bible Center, March 1, 2021. https://weekly.israelbiblecenter.com/prayer-mean-hebrew.

Longman, Tremper, III. *Book of Ecclesiastes*. Grand Rapids: Eerdmans, 1998.

Louw, Johannes E., and Eugene A. Nida. *Greek-English Lexicon of the New Testament: Based on Semantic Domains*. 2nd ed. New York: United Bible Societies, 1989.

Marshall, I. Howard. *The Acts of the Apostles*. 1915. Reprint, Grand Rapids: Eerdmans, 1991.

———. *The Epistles of John*. Grand Rapids: Eerdmans, 1978.

Martínez, Florentino García, and Eibert J. C. Tigchelaar. *The Dead Sea Scrolls Study Edition*. Vol. 2. Leiden: Brill, 1998.

McKinnon, Allan S. "Evil Spirits and Exorcism in the Bible." Academia, 2020. https://www.academia.edu/84812638/Evil_Spirits_and_Exorcism.

Missler, Chuck. "Mischievous Angels or Sethites?" Koinonia House, August 1, 1997. https://www.khouse.org/articles/1997/110/.

Morris, Robert. "Free Indeed Series: Set Free." Gateway Church, Dallas, Texas, January 1, 2014. https://www.gatewaypeople.com

/sermons/video/qdQnN4EWJ4A--free-indeed-set-free-pastor-robert
-morris?playlist=PLFgcIA8Y9FMDXa4LKQ_AdiiilReifMy56.

Mounce, William D. *Basics of Biblical Greek*. Grand Rapids: Zondervan, 1993.

Niehaus, Jeffrey J. *Biblical Theology*. Vol. 1, *The Common Grace Covenants*. Bellingham, WA: Lexham Press, 2014.

———. *Biblical Theology*. Vol. 2, *The Special Grace Covenants (Old
Testament)*. Bellingham, WA: Lexham Press, 2017.

———. *Biblical Theology*. Vol. 3, *The Special Grace Covenants (New
Testament)*. Bellingham, WA: Lexham Press, 2017.

———. "In the Wind of the Storm: Another Look at Genesis III 8."
Vetus Testamentum 44, no. 2 (1994): 263–67.

Ostberg, René. "Witching Hour." *Britannica*, November 30, 2022.
https://www.britannica.com/topic/witching-hour.

Person, Hara. "Hashkiveinu: Seeking Comfort and Protection through
the Night." My Jewish Learning. Accessed December 13, 2023.
https://www.myjewishlearning.com/article/hashkiveinu-seeking
-comfort-and-protection-through-the-night.

Sanders, Laura. "A Chemical Imbalance Doesn't Explain Depression.
So What Does?" *Science News*, February 24, 2023. https://www
.sciencenews.org/article/chemical-imbalance-explain-depression.

Schmitt, Rüdiger. "Demons, Demonology." In *The Encyclopedia of the
Bible and Its Reception*. Vol. 6 of *Dabbesheth—Dreams and Dream
Interpretation*. Berlin: de Gruyter, 2012.

Schwemer, Daniel. "Demons, Demonology." In *The Encyclopedia of
the Bible and Its Reception*. Vol. 6 of *Dabbesheth—Dreams and
Dream Interpretation*. Berlin: de Gruyter, 2012.

Shapiro, Marc. "Harnessing the Healing Power of Music." *Dome*.
Johns Hopkins Medicine, August 31, 2022. https://www.hopkin
smedicine.org/news/articles/2022/08/harnessing-the-healing-power
-of-music.

Smalley, Stephen S. *1, 2, 3 John*. Waco: Word, 1984.

Society of Saint Pius X. "The Didache: Introduction, Origin, and Re-
discovery." District of the USA, July 20, 2023. https://sspx.org/en
/news/didache-introduction-origin-and-rediscovery-29656.

Sorensen, Eric. "Demons, Demonology." In *The Encyclopedia of the Bible and Its Reception*. Vol. 6 of *Dabbesheth—Dreams and Dream Interpretation*. Berlin: de Gruyter, 2012.

Stuart, Douglas. *Old Testament Exegesis*. Philadelphia: Westminster, 1984.

Thayer, Joseph. *A Greek-English Lexicon of the New Testament* (abridged and revised Thayer Lexicon). Ontario: Online Bible Foundation, 1997.

Twelftree, Graham H. *Jesus the Exorcist: A Contribution to the Study of the Historical Jesus*. Peabody, MA: Hendrickson, 1993.

Unger, Merrill F. *Demons in the World Today*. Wheaton: Tyndale, 1971.

———. *What Demons Can Do to Saints*. Chicago: Moody, 1977.

"Why Humans Are Supposed to Sleep in Two 4-Hour Phases." Half as Interesting. August 12, 2021. https://youtube.com/watch?v=DKBXFf EPJyg&si=yOAgtx1ztBrpB9Dd.

Wiles, Jeremy. "Science Confirms Bible on Generational Curses." Conquer Series, June 22, 2022. https://conquerseries.com/science -confirms-bible-on-generational-curses.

Wilson, Marvin R. *Our Father Abraham: Jewish Roots of the Christian Faith*. 2nd ed. Grand Rapids: Eerdmans, 2021.

Wolff, Hans Walter. *Anthropology of the Old Testament*. Philadelphia: Fortress, 1974.

Zika, Charles. "Demons, Demonology." In *The Encyclopedia of the Bible and Its Reception*. Vol. 6 of *Dabbesheth—Dreams and Dream Interpretation*. Berlin: de Gruyter, 2012.